The iMovie '11 Project Book

Stuff you can
do with iMovie

D0557443

JEFF CARLSON

PEACHPIT PRESS

The iMovie '11 Project Book
Jeff Carlson

Peachpit Press
1249 Eighth Street
Berkeley, CA 94710
510/524-2178
510/524-2221 (fax)

Find us on the Web at: www.peachpit.com
To report errors, please send a note to errata@peachpit.com

Peachpit Press is a division of Pearson Education.
Copyright © 2011 by Jeff Carlson

Editor: Clifford Colby
Copyeditor: Scout Festa
Production editor: Lisa Brazieal
Compositor: Jeff Carlson
Indexer: Ann Rogers
Cover design: Mimi Heft
Cover compositor: Andreas deDanaan
Interior design: Peachpit Press

ISBN-13: 978-0-321-76819-3

ISBN-10:   0-321-76819-1

9 8 7 6 5 4 3 2 1

Printed and bound in the United States of America

*For Emily, Peter, Dana, David, Jennifer, Brett, Kellie,
Jeff, Christine, Michael, Suzanne, Ty, and Kimberly*

About the Author

Jeff Carlson gave up an opportunity to intern at a design firm during college because they really just wanted someone tall to play on their volleyball team. In the intervening years, he's been a designer and writer, authoring best-selling books on the Macintosh, Web design, video editing, and digital photography. His most recent book is *The iPad 2 Pocket Guide*. He's currently a columnist for the *Seattle Times*, a frequent contributor to *Macworld*, and a senior editor of *TidBITS* (www.tidbits.com), and he consumes almost too much coffee—*almost*. Find more information about him at jeffcarlson.com and neverenoughcoffee.com; follow him on Twitter at @jeffcarlson.

Acknowledgments

Writing this book about iMovie projects was, as I hope you can imagine, quite the project itself. It wouldn't have been a successful project at all without the assistance of the following people:

Cliff Colby guided the project from the beginning and listened to both my ideas and my concerns (the latter usually when I wasn't properly caffeinated).

Jeff Tolbert helped immeasurably by writing sections of Chapters 5 and 6 when I suddenly had to drop everything and write *The iPad 2 Pocket Guide* in the middle of production.

Lisa Brazieal is the coolest, calmest production editor on earth.

Ann Rogers turned my random writings into a useful index.

Scout Festa copyedited the book and kept me on my editing toes.

Kim and Ellie keep me sane and happy.

Agen Schmitz didn't actually work on this title, but he did update part of my iPad 2 book. I was so rushed to get it done that I didn't include him in the acknowledgments for that book, making me the worst-colleague-ever-who-now-owes-Agen-several-beers.

Contents

Introduction

I love that I've been able to write a book about *projects* in iMovie.

Editing video, after all, is a project in many ways. It often requires a good deal of time and attention to detail. It's something you elect to do, probably in your spare time, because you want to document what happened at an event, or preserve memories, or communicate something in a way that text or photos alone are incapable of doing.

And I also love that I've been able to write a book about projects in *iMovie*. If you plucked a much younger me from the days when I first began editing video and showed me today's iMovie, my brain would have had trouble processing what I was seeing (not to mention dealing with the fact that somehow I had been pulled through time). For as little as $15, or free when you buy a new Mac, you have the capability to edit high-definition video in real time, using a friendly interface that genuinely makes editing fun.

And let's not even speculate how my brain would have reacted to editing HD video on the iPad, using iMovie for iOS.

Most of all, I love living in a time where these capabilities are available to millions of people who are willing to set aside some time and creativity. The future really is the best project.

About the iMovie Projects

I call it *The iMovie '11 Project Book* because I present the information in the form of projects: simple tasks you can do quickly that highlight an important concept or technique, and which you can build upon for your own video editing projects.

I've divided the book into the following seven chapters:

- **A Primer on Shooting Video.** It doesn't matter the equipment, the experience, or the budget—shooting poor footage leads to mediocre movies. Here are some tips for improving the experience in the field.

- **iMovie Fundamentals.** Learn the building blocks of importing, editing, and working with features such as iMovie's movie trailers.

- **Organize Your Video Library.** Video projects start with lots of clips, which can easily get lost or overlooked when it's time to start cutting them together. Learn how to store, move, and mark footage, and how to use keywords to find clips quickly.

- **iMovie Beyond the Basics.** Replace clips, build a photo slideshow, correct color, adjust audio...find out how much more iMovie can do to make your video projects more interesting and enjoyable.

- **Creative iMovie Projects.** Using the skills you've learned, stretch iMovie's creativity by making a travel highlights movie, a sports highlights movie, a music video, green-screen special effects, and a soundtrack using GarageBand.

- **Share Your Movies.** Don't let your videos sit inert on a hard drive. Burn them to DVDs, share them on the Web, or transfer them to an iOS device, including the Apple TV.

- **Edit Video on the iPad, iPhone, or iPod touch.** You no longer have to wait until you get back to your Mac to edit video. Learn all about working with the iMovie for iOS app.

Although I've included a lot of great information, this book isn't an encyclopedic look at iMovie. Jump in, enjoy yourself, and create something.

A Note About Conventions

When describing a command, I often need to direct you to a menu item. Since your eyes would glaze over if every mention was like, "Choose the Large item under the Viewer submenu of the Window menu," I use a hierachical shortcut that follows how you'd click the menu items: "Choose Window > Viewer > Large".

I also frequently mention settings in iMovie's preferences window. Rather than direct you to the command each time (choose iMovie > Preferences), I'm more likely to just write "In iMovie's preferences..."

In terms of interacting with the software, the convention for describing the arrow you manipulate around the screen is a "mouse pointer," even though in many cases you may be using a laptop trackpad or Apple's Magic Trackpad instead of a mouse. Similarly, I talk about "clicking the mouse button," which translates to single-clicking the button on the mouse or trackpad.

Lastly, I often refer to the "contextual menu," which is a pop-up menu containing commands that apply to the element you're working with. To access the contextual menu, either hold the Control key and click the mouse button or right-click the mouse.

Getting iMovie '11

Unless you haven't purchased a Mac in over a decade, you currently own a version of iMovie. Apple has shipped iLife (which also includes iPhoto, GarageBand, iDVD, and iWeb) free with every new Mac since 2003, and has included iMovie on new Macs since iMovie 1.0 appeared in 1999. Look for iMovie in your Applications folder; it may also already be in your Dock. However, I can't automatically assume you have iMovie '11, the latest version, introduced in 2010. Most of the material in this book still applies if you're running iMovie '08 or iMovie '09.

However, if your latest version is iMovie HD 6 or earlier, nothing will be familiar. Apple completely rewrote iMovie for the '08 version, setting aside the old program in favor of a new approach. iMovie HD still works on modern Macs, although it's no longer actively supported by Apple.

There are three ways to get iMovie '11:

- **Buy a new Mac.** This can be an awfully expensive way to buy a piece of software, but you get some very nice hardware thrown in with the deal. Seriously, if you're contemplating a new Mac purchase anyway, the most recent Macs offer powerful processors, fast graphics processing (which can improve performance in iMovie), and the latest version of the iLife suite.

- **Buy iLife at retail.** For $49 from Apple, or from Amazon.com and other resellers, you get a boxed version of the suite on a DVD.

- **Buy iMovie from the Mac App Store.** Introduced in late 2010, the Mac App Store is an application on your Mac that lets you purchase software as direct downloads from Apple. (If you don't have the App Store application, make sure you're running Mac OS X 10.6.6 or later; from the Apple menu (), choose Software Update and install the latest version.) What's great about the Mac App Store is that you can buy iMovie '11 by itself for just $15. iPhoto '11 and Garage-Band '11 are also available for the same price, but iWeb and iDVD—which haven't been updated since iLife '09—are not. If you're looking to upgrade from iLife '08 or earlier, go for the boxed set.

1

A Primer on Shooting Video

The capability to record motion pictures has been around for about a century, and the current state of the art—high-definition video that average consumers can afford—is really just a blip in that timeline. One thing has remained constant, however, whether you're shooting with a feature-film camera or an iPhone:

Get the best source video you can.

No amount of postprocessing can resurrect poor-quality footage, unless maybe you have millions of dollars at your disposal or your initials are I.L.M. So, before we jump into how iMovie works and the projects you can undertake, let's look at the equipment needed to capture video and learn some basic shooting principles that will improve the original—and often irreplaceable—footage.

Gear Up

If you haven't followed the camcorder market for a couple of years, you'll be forgiven if suddenly everything looks different. Fairly recently, most every digital camcorder stored its footage on magnetic DV tape cassettes. Now, go to an electronics store and you'll discover that the market is dominated by tapeless cameras that record directly to memory—built-in memory, storage cards, or small internal hard disks. Or, don't go: You may have a perfectly acceptable video recorder in your pocket right now—your cell phone.

This section is an overview of what's out there now and is by no means exhaustive. The video-recording field is vast, catering to high-end professionals shooting feature films and television shows on expensive HD cameras, as well as everyday folks who want to be able to capture birthday parties, weekend vacations, and school projects.

Types of cameras

The definition of a "camcorder" has broadened dramatically. Nearly every digital still camera can shoot decent video these days, and the latest digital SLR cameras are being used to replace much costlier video gear in professional productions. At the other end of the spectrum, portable Flip cameras make recording a one-button operation, and the iPhone 4 captures HD video, so you no longer need to carry a separate device dedicated solely to shooting video.

Since iMovie is a consumer application, I'll assume that if you're considering a camera such as the Red One ($25,000 for the body, without lenses), you already know the field and don't need a briefing from me.

Camcorders

Most digital camcorders (**Figure 1.1**) record to solid-state memory, usually SDHC cards or built-in memory chips, with a few that record to an internal hard disk. (See "Understand video formats," just ahead, for more on the files that are stored.) They're also geared toward video capture by offering features such as good telephoto zoom ranges, optical image stabilization, and large LCD screens.

Figure 1.1
Most camcorders are small enough to hold in your hand, but packed with video features.

If you want more control over the video you shoot (and are willing to pay for it), look for the following features:

- **Manual focus ring.** Most camcorders offer a manual focus mode, but you must press buttons or manipulate onscreen sliders to set the focus. A real focus ring around the lens is much easier to use.

- **Three CCDs.** For better color fidelity, look for a camera that has three CCDs (charge-coupled devices), the sensors that record incoming light from the lens. Most cameras include just one CCD to capture light, whereas a three-CCD camera independently records red, green, and blue colors.

- **Hot shoe.** A connector at the top of the camcorder delivers power and data between accessories such as video lights and microphones.

- **Audio terminals.** Connect microphones and headphones that can be placed anywhere.

 It's possible to buy a camcorder that records to DV tape, but these are the last days for the format. iMovie will import footage from tape but doesn't offer a way to write a finished movie back to it (a feature in old versions of iMovie, when making a tape of your movie and then connecting the camcorder to a television was one of the few ways to play the movie for others).

Flip cameras

The popular Flip cameras are the size of a large cell phone, yet they can shoot decent HD video. The appeal of a Flip is simplicity: Forget about manual focus, white balance settings, or any other fluff. Just point the camera at your subject, press the large red Record button, and...well, that's it. You can review your footage and delete clips, but it's hard to get a sense of quality from the tiny LCD screen. When it's time to offload the video, a USB plug flips out of the top to connect to your computer. Similar cameras are also offered by Kodak, Panasonic, Samsung, and others.

DSLR and still cameras

Until a few years ago, there was a large gap between camcorders and DSLRs (digital single-lens reflex, or still cameras with removable lenses)—they performed completely different tasks: video and still imagery. Now, Hollywood cinematographers and special-effects houses are using top-of-the-line Canon and Nikon DSLRs (**Figure 1.2**) to shoot video because they're vastly less expensive than high-end professional gear and the quality is often just as good.

Figure 1.2
Consumer DSLRs have turned into formidable video cameras.

DSLRs have the advantage of shooting with the full range of lenses that photographers have been using for years, and which can produce smooth and shallow depth of field that is more difficult to achieve in most camcorders. On the other hand, they're still primarily still cameras, so getting them to function like camcorders takes extra gear and persistence. For example, many DSLRs lack manual exposure controls for video and have slow (or non-existent) autofocus.

If you're taking the DSLR route, I highly recommend the book *From Still to Motion: A photographer's guide to creating video with your DSLR*, by James Ball, Robbie Carman, Matt Gottshalk, and Richard Harrington.

Surprisingly, you may not need the power and expense of a DSLR to get good video. Pretty much every consumer digital camera can shoot video, and now there are models that produce great HD video, too (**Figure 1.3**). Even fewer controls are available, but if you're more likely to shoot video if the camera is already at hand, a still camera will get the shot.

Figure 1.3
The PowerShot G12 is an excellent little still camera and captures high-quality HD video.

Cell phones

If I had mentioned cellular phones as a video source just a couple of years ago, you'd have laughed in my face. Sure, the phone and its camera are handy, but only if you enjoy watching shapeless blobs of pixels march across the screen. As technology has advanced and components have shrunk, however, we now have cameras like the iPhone 4 that capture surprisingly good HD video. And soon, I'm sure, I won't feel the need to add "surprisingly" when I mention it.

Understand video formats

I've thrown around terms like "HD" and "DV" loosely thus far, so what am I talking about when discussing video formats? Unfortunately, there isn't one universal video format; instead, iMovie supports output from cameras that offer combinations of image sizes, format types, and image compression.

Image size

Usually when someone is talking about "HD," they're referring to the number of pixels in each frame of video. The more pixels that are available, the higher the resolution of the image, which produces a picture that's a better quality than SD, or standard definition, video. **Figure 1.4** compares the most common sizes.

Figure 1.4
HD uses much more image information than standard-definition video. Also note that HD features a 16:9 widescreen aspect ratio, while SD uses the television standard 4:3 ratio.

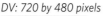
DV: 720 by 480 pixels

HD 720p: 1280 by 720 pixels

HD 1080i/1080p: 1920 by 1080 pixels

note You'll notice that the width for DV is 720 pixels, which should make the frame wider than it is. The DV format actually uses tall *rectangular* pixels, not square ones. Other standard-definition (SD) formats, such as those captured by digital still cameras, record video with square pixels at 640 by 480 pixels.

HD cameras record footage in two varieties, progressive and interlaced, which are represented by the "p" and "i" notations in the figure. So, "1080p" indicates that the video image is 1080 pixels high, and every frame of video is captured in its entirety, the way each frame of film is recorded.

By contrast, "1080i" footage is also 1080 pixels high, but the frames are interlaced. Interlacing is a technique where every other horizontal line of a frame is recorded. For example, the even-numbered lines are recorded in one pass, and then the odd-numbered lines are recorded in the next pass. When you play back the footage, it speeds past your eyes fast enough to convince your brain that you're looking at a single frame (**Figure 1.5**).

Figure 1.5
Interlacing actually stores about half of the image information for each frame. (Interlacing is also the way most televisions operate.)

Progressive frame

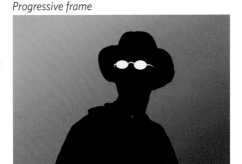

Interlaced frame   *Next interlaced frame*

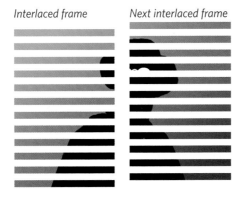

Formats and compression

Many HD camcorders encode video as AVCHD (Advanced Video Codec High Definition), which uses MPEG-4 compression to reduce the size of the captured data so it will easily fit onto a memory card. AVCHD is quite impressive considering that the camera is literally throwing away image information to reduce the file sizes.

You'll probably also see camcorders that record video as HDV (High Definition Video—really, who comes up with these boring names?), which uses MPEG-2 compression and interlacing to keep file sizes under control.

When you get into the realm of Flip cameras, DSLRs, and digital still cameras, the formats are more varied. Some cameras save native QuickTime files with H.264 encoding; some record to a new format called iFrame; some use just MPEG-4 encoding.

 Apple maintains an ongoing list of cameras it has tested for compatibility with iMovie at help.apple.com/imovie/cameras/. If you're thinking of buying a new camera, it's worth checking out the list for options. Also check out Apple's list of formats supported by QuickTime (support.apple.com/kb/HT3775); if QuickTime supports it, iMovie does, too.

Go Shooting

You'd think that capturing video is just a matter of turning the camera on and pointing it in the right direction. In many situations, I'm sure that's fine, but a little forethought and preparation can help you get good footage, not just acceptable footage.

Capture good video

The techniques I discuss here are suggestions, not hard and fast rules. What's important is to be aware of these types of situations when you're shooting, so you have the presence of mind to think, "This shot might be more dramatic if I focus close on this foreground object and make the background blurry." I say this because it's one of the things I struggle with most when shooting video. I get so focused on "getting the shot" that I don't immediately consider composition or how stable the camera is. It requires practice to take a deep breath, check your surroundings, and then compose your shot.

Hold steady

Shaky footage is the hallmark of amateur video. Even when you see handheld shots in a feature film, the camera motion is different than what most people produce when holding a camcorder. Mostly this is due to the size of the camera: Smaller, lighter cameras are more difficult to hold steady and are more susceptible to minor bumps and jostles (especially when you're shooting at the camera's maximum zoom setting). iMovie's image stabilization feature can help correct for bumpy video, but the results depend on how much motion there is, and even what type of camera was used (see "Stabilize Shaky Footage Project" in Chapter 4).

So, as much as possible, keep the camera steady. One way to do this is to set the camera on a tripod or monopod (a single leg with a screw on which the camera is attached). I also like the flexible Gorillapod tripods (**Figure 1.6**) made by Joby (www.joby.com).

Figure 1.6
The Gorillapod not only acts as a tripod, it can be wrapped around objects for greater stability.

If you still want to shoot handheld, do this: Tuck your elbows into your sides for more support under the camera, and swivel your torso when you need to pan left or right. You can also lean against solid structures like door frames or walls for extra stability while shooting.

Compose shots using the rule of thirds

Is everyone in your video planted squarely in the center of the frame? You were probably taught to center your subject when taking pictures, but adjusting the composition slightly makes for much more interesting shots. An easy way to accomplish this is to use the "rule of thirds": Imagine your view is split into three sections wide and three sections tall, and balance the subjects into one of the outer areas (**Figure 1.7**). Some cameras offer an overlay onto the viewfinder or LCD screen that helps you compose the shot. This isn't to say nothing should appear in the middle of the screen; only that a variety of compositions will yield better footage.

Figure 1.7
The bridge appears in the left third portion of the frame, balancing the open sky and marina on the right.

When people or objects are moving in the frame, position them so the viewer sees where they're going (**Figure 1.8**) instead of heading out of the frame.

Be aware of everything in the camera's field of view. It's easy to focus your attention on the main subject, but if something distracting or disturbing is happening elsewhere in the frame, your viewer is likely to pay more attention to the distraction.

Figure 1.8
As someone is walking across the frame, give them space to move toward.

Depth of field

Most camcorders are great about automatically focusing on the objects in your scene, but they tend to focus as much as possible. "Depth of field" refers to the distance between the camera and the object furthest from the lens. One technique for drawing attention to something in a shot is to use selective focus, making an object in the foreground tack-sharp while the background is blurry—also known as having a shallow depth of field. This task is made easier by shooting with a DSLR through a lens with a large aperture (**Figure 1.9**).

Figure 1.9
This video was shot with a Nikon D90 DSLR using a 50mm f/1.8 lens to take advantage of a shallow depth of field.

You can achieve a similar effect with a camcorder by doing the following:

1. Position the camera as far away from your subject as possible.

2. Use the camcorder's zooming controls to zoom in close to the subject.

3. Set the manual focus so that the subject is clear.

 Speaking of focus, if you're performing an interview or other situation where the camera is fixed in one position and the focus is on one person or stationary object, switch to manual focus. Camcorders in autofocus mode are constantly checking focus, so the smallest movement from your subject could cause the camera to adjust focus, causing an effect where the screen seems to be "bouncing."

Capture good audio

Don't forget about audio! Video shooting and editing is primarily a visual activity, but if the audio portion of your footage is muddy, the work you put into making great images is diminished.

That said, in many situations you may not have much of a choice. Camcorder microphones vary in quality and are all confined to the camera itself. That doesn't help much if you're shooting something a moderate distance away. If you want to improve the quality of the audio you capture, there are a few things you can do.

Use an external microphone

On a movie set, the primary microphone is suspended from a boom over the actors' heads, held aloft by an impressively strong man or woman who keeps their arms up most of the day. The idea is to get a microphone as close as possible to the dialogue, and away from the noisy camera (or camera operator).

For regular shooting, consider purchasing a directional microphone (provided your camera will accept it). Companies such as Røde (www.rodemic.com) sell shotgun microphones that pick up audio from only what they're pointed at, not from noise behind or to the side.

If you do a lot of interviews, or you do podcasts where you're the main subject, consider buying a lavalier microphone that clips onto a shirt or tie (**Figure 1.10**). Wireless variants are also available.

Figure 1.10
A simple clip-on lavalier microphone can greatly increase the quality of your recorded audio.

Record with a set of headphones

You won't know for certain what your camera's microphone is picking up without hearing it through a set of headphones (**Figure 1.11**). Your ears pick out some sounds and ignore others, a feature most camcorders do not have. Using any inexpensive headphones will work fine—what's important is that you hear what the camera hears while recording, not in iMovie later when there's little that can be done about the quality.

Figure 1.11
Monitor the audio your camcorder is recording.

tip Take a few minutes to record...nothing. Or rather, make a point of capturing a few minutes' worth of ambient noise, what an environment sounds like when nothing else is going on. This is important even in "silent" rooms, because although your ears may register quiet, there's still quite a lot of sound occurring. You can use that neutral audio later, in the event you need to minimize an unexpected loud sound (like a sneeze off-camera).

Get plenty of coverage

You're going to shoot more video than you'll ever use in iMovie, and that's fantastic. It's much better to have a surplus of footage to work with than to scramble to find a shot that doesn't exist. Linger on scenes, don't just stop recording once the "action" has ended. You can always omit the footage when you build your movie project.

In fact, get into the habit of shooting things that catch your eye that may have nothing to do with the main focus of your movie. A few artistic shots of the flower gardens outside a ceremony can make for a nice cutaway or maybe a great background on which you hang the movie's title (**Figure 1.12**).

Figure 1.12
I shot this leaf against the sky and framed it specifically to use it as a title.

Types of coverage

When shooting a feature-length motion picture, a director will use multiple camera setups to shoot as much coverage as possible. So in one scene, the camera may shoot both actors in the frame, each actor from one or more different positions, and various combinations of points of view. The goal is to present a scene in the edited movie where the camera position is integral to the scene's mood or content.

- **Establishing shot.** This is usually an overview shot that's wide enough to let the viewer know the setting and which characters inhabit the scene. It can be a sign reading "Welcome to Twin Falls," a shot of someone's house, or a shot of a room. The important thing is that the establishing shot provides a physical geography of where objects appear.

  (This technique is used to great effect in dozens of movies and television shows: you see an establishing shot of the Chicago skyline and assume that the action takes place there, even though the actual filming took place in Vancouver.)

- **Medium shot.** Most shots end up as variations of medium shots. Generally, this shot is large enough to frame the torsos of two or three people, although it could range from a shot of a single person to half of a room (**Figure 1.13**).

Figure 1.13
A medium shot is typically close enough to include two or three people.

- **Close-up.** The screen is filled with part of a person or object. Close-ups usually show a person's head and shoulders, but they can also push in closer (known as an extreme close-up) so you see only the person's eyes. Other examples of close-ups include shots of a person's hands, or of any object that occupies the entire frame.

- **Cut-away shot.** Sometimes referred to as B-roll footage, cut-aways are shots of associated objects or scenes that aren't necessarily part of the central action in a scene. An example would be the view from a ship traveling through a passage, which cuts away to a shot of the darkening sky, but then returns to the ship safely emerging from the passage. Cut-aways often prove invaluable when you need to cover up a few frames of a glitch or when cutting and shortening interviews.

- **In points and out points.** If possible, give yourself some shots that can be used to enter or exit a scene, sometimes known as in points and out points. For example, if you're shooting an interview and your subject has just declared his intention to walk on Mars, don't immediately stop recording. Hold the camera on him as he finishes speaking, then perhaps pan down to his desk where a model of his rocket ship is mounted.

tip Don't forget to take visual notes; after all, your camera is an ideal record-keeper. If you're traveling, make a point of getting shots of important signs, markers, or waypoints so you have a geographic idea of where the scenes took place when you're far away, hunkered down editing in front of your computer.

tip Remember, shooting video isn't like shooting still photos—you can't turn the camera 90 degrees to get a portrait-oriented shot, because video always appears horizontal. I've seen people turn the camera to get an entire waterfall into a shot, only to realize at home that the water is falling from left to right. It *is* possible to rotate the footage in iMovie, but it's much better to keep the camera horizontal when you're shooting.

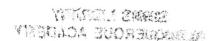

2

iMovie Fundamentals

iMovie is designed to be easy to use, but the interface is intimidating at a first look. This is especially true if you've previously used other software such as the original iMovie HD, Final Cut, or Adobe Premiere. So, although it's possible to sit down the first time and jump right in, you'll benefit from understanding the fundamentals of how iMovie operates.

This chapter sets the groundwork for the projects that follow in the rest of the book. You may already know some of the material, in which case I urge you to skim these pages and pick out any tips or techniques that may be new to you. If this is your first time using iMovie, follow along in this chapter and soon, with the basics under control, you'll be ready to tackle the other projects with confidence.

Get Acquainted with iMovie

Even short video projects take time to edit. When you become comfortable working in iMovie's window, you'll forget about the parts and pieces and be able to focus on what's important: your video.

Tour iMovie's interface

Nearly everything in iMovie happens in its main window: create a new project, choose which footage to use, add clips to your movie, edit it all together, and more. Like knowing how to navigate your living room furniture in the dark, you'll soon know where everything is in iMovie without thinking about it. Until then, here's a quick guide to the main working areas (**Figure 2.1**). I go into more detail about how each one works as we progress through the book.

Figure 2.1
The main areas of iMovie's interface:

A   Project Library and Project browser

B   Viewer

C   Toolbar

D   Event Library

E   Event browser

F   Other browsers area (Photos browser shown)

The Project Library and Project browser

The upper-left area of the window is shared by the Project Library and the Project browser. The Project Library lists all video editing projects and movie trailers you've created. Double-clicking a project pushes the library out of the way to reveal the Project browser, where you assemble and edit the movie (**Figure 2.2**).

Figure 2.2
The Project Library (left) and Project browser (right)

> **tip** The View menu includes options to display content in the Event Library by hard disk, by month, and by day.

The Project browser deserves extra scrutiny for how your project appears. Traditional video-editing timelines scroll left to right off the screen, but in iMovie, the project is structured more like a paragraph of text. The video starts at the upper-left, proceeds left-to-right along the first row, and then jumps down to the next row (**Figure 2.3**). This approach lets you view more of your project at once. (It's possible to regain a timeline, however; see "Switch to a 'traditional' timeline," later in this chapter.)

Figure 2.3
A project is organized in multiple rows like a paragraph of text.

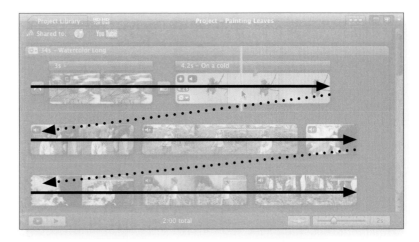

The Viewer

The Viewer is the live preview of video that you play back or that appears under your mouse pointer when it hovers over a clip. In some circumstances, the Viewer is also a place to edit; for example, that's where you type text for titles and adjust the appearance of imported photos.

The toolbar

Most of the editing controls, plus an audio levels indicator, appear in the center toolbar.

Here's one of the best things you can do in iMovie *right now*: Open the program's preferences (choose iMovie > Preferences, or press Command-, [comma]) and enable the Show Advanced Tools option. That unlocks additional features, such as applying keywords or performing green-screen edits, that are otherwise hidden.

The Event Library and Event browser

Each batch of footage you import is organized into a new event in the Event Library. Selecting an event displays its video to the right in the Event browser, enabling you to see which clips are available.

Other browsers

Normally, the browsers shown to the right of the Event browser in Figure 2.1 are hidden to give you more room to view clips. But when it's time to add a song, photo, title, transition, map, or background, clicking the buttons to the right of the toolbar brings up the appropriate browsers.

Preview and play video

A common element in all video editors is the *playhead*, which indicates the frame you're currently viewing. In iMovie, the playhead is a red vertical bar that spans the height of a clip (**Figure 2.4**).

What's different about iMovie's playhead is that it appears whenever the mouse pointer moves over a clip—regardless of whether that clip is in a movie you're editing or in the Event browser. As you move the pointer across a clip, the Viewer displays the footage beneath it, an action called *skimming*.

Figure 2.4
The Viewer displays the frame under the playhead.

Playhead

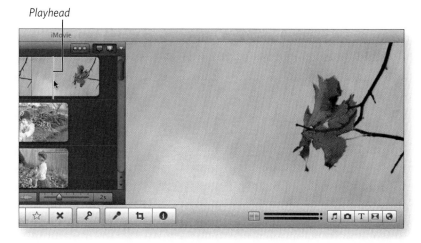

To play video in real time, you have a few options:

- Position the playhead where you want to begin playing, and press the spacebar.

 - To play a project from the beginning, click the Play Project from Beginning button at the lower-left corner of the Project Library.

    Similarly, you can play events in the Event browser by clicking the Play Selected Events from Beginning button at the lower-left corner of the Event Library.

 - To play a project or an event from the beginning in full-screen mode, click the appropriate Play Full Screen button.

 Forget the buttons: Press the \ (backslash) key to start playing a project or event from the beginning.

Customize iMovie's appearance

When you sit down to work, do you subtly adjust your workspace to make it more comfortable? iMovie includes a few adjustments that help you focus on tasks and decide how much of a clip's thumbnails to view.

Adjust the size of clip thumbnails

Drag the thumbnail size slider to increase or decrease the thumbnails in both the Project browser and the Event browser (**Figure 2.5**).

Figure 2.5
Small thumbnails (left) and large thumbnails (right).

Adjust the number of frames per thumbnail

The whole point of displaying clips as thumbnails is to better view your project at a glance. Sometimes you want to get an overview of the movie, where each clip shows a single thumbnail; at other times, you'll want to see more thumbnails per clip to determine the point at which some action occurs. For example, if a friend in your video does something interesting within a long clip, you may not see it (or easily locate the clip) if just one thumbnail image is visible.

Drag the clips size slider to set how much time each thumbnail represents, as indicated to the right of the slider (**Figure 2.6**). The Project browser and Event browser each have their own slider.

Figure 2.6
This 5.5-second clip appears as three thumbnails when the clips size slider is set to 2 seconds.

Change the size of the Viewer

Although this feature focuses on the size of the Viewer, its real purpose is to provide more working space for the other main areas of the interface. Choose Window > Viewer, and then choose one of the preset sizes:

- Small (or press Command-8) makes more room for the Event browser, for when you're sorting through your raw footage.

- Medium (Command-9) balances the sizes of the Project browser, the Viewer, and the Event browser by positioning the toolbar in the middle of the window.

- Large (Command-0) expands the area used by the Project browser, for when you're editing your movie and don't need to focus on events.

You can also click anywhere within the toolbar and drag it up or down.

I'm a big fan of working with multiple monitors, especially when editing video. If you have an external display connected to your Mac, you can use it as the Viewer and free up space on your main display to show more of the Project browser (Figure 2.7). Choose Window > Viewer on Other Display. (If that option doesn't appear, make sure the Show Advanced Tools option is enabled in iMovie's preferences.)

Figure 2.7
iMovie on my main display (left) and the Viewer on a secondary monitor (right).

Switch to a "traditional" timeline

When Apple introduced iMovie '08, the program was completely different than versions of iMovie that had come before. (Literally: It was a brand new program that inherited the "iMovie" name.) People long accustomed to editing a project in a single horizontal strip at the bottom of the screen had to adjust to the multi-row layout of the Project browser. Largely for this reason, a lot of folks chose to stick with iMovie HD 6 or investigate other options such as Final Cut Express.

After three versions, the "new" iMovie finally brings back a traditional timeline used by the "old" iMovie and most other video editors for those who want it. Apple calls it the Single-Row View.

Switching to a traditional timeline

1. In the Project browser, click the Single-Row View button to extend the project's clips beyond the left and right edges of the browser (**Figure 2.8**).

Figure 2.8
The Viewer displays the frame under the playhead.

Single-Row View button

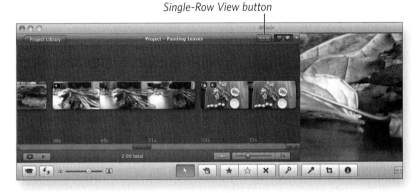

2. Click the Swap Events and Projects button to move the Project browser to the bottom of the window.

Add Video to Your iMovie Library

Now that you have a general idea of how to move around iMovie's window, it's time to get practical. To start editing video, you must first import raw footage.

Import video from a memory-based camera

The majority of camcorders today record video directly to memory, which can include memory cards, internal memory chips, or a hard drive embedded within the camera. iMovie gives you the option of importing all available clips, or just the clips you choose.

 note **Even though nearly all digital still cameras now capture video, iMovie doesn't recognize them as import sources. (Notable exceptions are the iPhone, iPad, and iPod touch.) Instead, first bring the clips into iPhoto or Aperture, or save them to your hard disk, and import them into iMovie from there (described a few pages ahead).**

Importing video from a memory-based camera:

1. Connect the camera to your Mac; if it's a supported device and iMovie is already open, the Import dialog automatically appears. You can also click the Import button on the toolbar to open the dialog.

2. To preview any clip, click it and press the Play button beneath the dialog's viewer (**Figure 2.9**).

Figure 2.9
The Import dialog.

Mode switch   Play button

3. If you want to import all clips, make sure the mode switch at the lower-left corner is set to Automatic; skip to step 5. Or, set it to Manual to choose which clips to import.

4. Mark the checkboxes below each clip that you want to import. If you need only a few, clicking the Uncheck All button first and then making your selections can save a little time.

5. Click the Import button, which will read either "Import All" or "Import Checked," depending on what's selected.

6. In the next dialog that appears, specify where the video will be stored (typically your Mac's hard drive). Also, decide whether the footage will appear in an existing Event, or create a new Event for the clips (**Figure 2.10**). If the footage spans several days, iMovie can create separate Events for each day; click the "Split days into new Events" checkbox.

Figure 2.10
Every new clip must be in an existing Event or a new one.

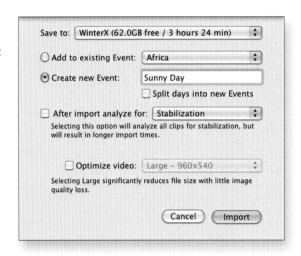

Save to: WinterX (62.0GB free / 3 hours 24 min)

○ Add to existing Event: Africa

⦿ Create new Event: Sunny Day

☐ Split days into new Events

☐ After import analyze for: Stabilization
Selecting this option will analyze all clips for stabilization, but will result in longer import times.

☐ Optimize video: Large – 960x540
Selecting Large significantly reduces file size with little image quality loss.

Cancel   Import

7. Two additional options are available:

- To have iMovie determine how to apply stabilization or locate people, enable the "After import analyze for" checkbox. The pop-up menu lets you select Stabilization, People, or both.

  This option will significantly increase the import time, adding *several hours* to the process if you're bringing in a lot of footage. The advantage of analyzing at import is that you can enable stabilization or locate people instantly while you're editing, versus waiting each time you want to apply the effect. If you want to choose this route, import the footage just before going to bed or before you'll be away from the computer for hours.

- The "Optimize video" option does two things to HD clips in the interest of ensuring smooth playback: It converts the video files to AIC (Apple Intermediate Codec), iMovie's preferred editing format, and it optionally resizes the clips' dimensions to 960 by 540 pixels to reduce the file sizes.

If you choose the Large - 960x540 option in the pop-up menu, you most likely won't notice much difference from the Full - Original Size option, but iMovie will perform better during playback and editing.

Also, if your camcorder records in AVCHD or HDV format, the footage must be converted to AIC regardless, so you'll need to choose either the Large or Full option.

 **I'm of two minds about whether to import the Large or Full size. On one hand, I don't want to just throw away my original video by downsizing it. But on the other hand, most of what I shoot works equally well at 960 by 540. If you want to preserve your original footage (think of it as a digital negative), you can either make sure the option is disabled at import, or, if the footage is AVCHD, click the Archive All button that appears in the Import window. The archive feature copies the footage from your camera to your hard disk without converting it. The archive doesn't appear in iMovie—you still need to import and convert it—but a backup of the original clips is retained. The archive feature is also good if you want to quickly unload the camera's memory so you can shoot more.**

8. Click the Import button to transfer the clips and add them to iMovie's library.

9. Click Done to exit the Import window. The clips appear in the Event browser (**Figure 2.11**).

Figure 2.11
Imported clips appear in the Event you specified.

Access video from iPhoto or Aperture

Currently, the best video camera I own is a Canon PowerShot G12—a compact *still* camera that shoots great HD video. iMovie doesn't recognize it as a camcorder, however, but iPhoto and Aperture both accept video files as well as photo files, and iMovie can grab the clips directly from those photo applications. (If you use a non-Apple program such as Adobe Photoshop Lightroom to organize your photo library, you'll need to export videos to the hard disk and then import them into iMovie as stand-alone video files.)

Accessing video from iPhoto or Aperture

1. In iMovie's Event Library, click iPhoto Videos or, if you own Aperture, Aperture Videos. Clips appear in the Event browser, grouped by date and Event (**Figure 2.12**).

Figure 2.12
Access videos stored in your iPhoto or Aperture libraries.

2. From here, you can add footage directly to a project and start editing it; as far as iMovie is concerned, video in iPhoto or Aperture is as much a part of the library as video imported into an iMovie Event.

    You can also select clips and drag them to an iMovie Event. I often do this when I want to keep clips together that were shot using different cameras. Having them in one iMovie Event is easier than checking iPhoto or Aperture for the clips I need.

Import video from a tape-based camcorder

Not so long ago, consumer digital camcorders recorded only to small cassette tapes. Now, nearly everything on the market records to memory chips, but iMovie continues to support importing footage from tape-based camcorders.

 Although iMovie can import video from a tape-based camcorder, it cannot write footage back to tape. That used to be one way to share a movie you edited, after which you'd connect the camera to a TV for playback. But with the Web, iDVD, and other methods of sharing video, Apple determined that writing to tape is now outdated.

Importing from a tape-based camcorder

1. Connect the camera to your computer and switch the camera's mode switch to Play/VCR (or similar).

 2. In iMovie, click the Import button to open the Import window.

3. If you want to import all footage on the tape, set the mode switch to Automatic. Otherwise, set it to Manual.

4. Use the playback controls in the toolbar to locate the section of tape where you want to begin recording (**Figure 2.13**).

Figure 2.13
Previewing a clip from a tape-based camcorder.

Playback controls

5. When you're ready to capture the footage, click the Import button.

6. In the next dialog that appears, select a location and Event name for the incoming video. You can also choose to analyze the footage after importing (see my long-winded explanation of this option four pages back for details).

7. Click the Stop button to halt import and save the captured clip to your library.

8. Click Done to close the Import window. The clips appear in the Event browser.

Import video from the hard disk

Video files that don't come from a camcorder can be imported from the Finder. Those could include movies saved out of a program like Lightroom (which can't talk directly to iMovie), as well as AVCHD archives you created using iMovie in lieu of converting and importing the footage into the Event Library.

Importing video from disk

1. Choose File > Import > Movies.

2. In the dialog that appears, locate the file you wish to import.

3. Choose or create an Event where the footage will show up in the Event Library.

4. Decide whether or not to optimize the video, and choose a size in the Optimize Video pop-up menu.

5. If you want to keep the original file in place after importing it, choose the Copy Files radio button at the bottom of the dialog. A copy is added to your library. The alternative is to choose Move Files, which first makes a copy of the video and then deletes the original. (If you've opted to optimize the clip, the file will be copied, not moved, regardless of the setting.)

 To import a camera archive, choose File > Import > Camera Archive and locate the folder containing the raw AVCHD files. Then, follow the steps outlined earlier in "Import video from a memory-based camera."

Create a New iMovie Project

With a library full of raw material, you can now start editing the video into a movie. When you create a new movie project, you can start with a blank slate or choose one of iMovie's themes to add pre-made animations, titles, and transitions. (You can also create movie trailers here, which I cover in more detail later in "Create a Movie Trailer.")

1. Choose File > New Project, or press Command-N. You can also click the New Project button in the Project browser.

2. In the dialog that appears, type a project name in the Name field (**Figure 2.14**).

Figure 2.14
Creating a new project.

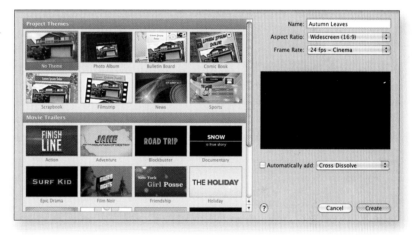

Don't worry about the Aspect Ratio or Frame Rate pop-up menus right now. The project applies these settings based on the first clip you add. You can change the settings later if you need to.

3. By default, a new project has no theme, but you can click one under the Project Themes heading to preview how it will look.

4. If you'd like iMovie to automatically add transitions between every clip in a project without a theme, click the "Automatically add" checkbox and choose a transition style from the pop-up menu. If a theme is applied, that control lets you opt to automatically add transitions and titles or leave them out (to be added manually later).

5. Click the Create button to create the empty project.

Add Clips to the Movie

Before we talk about adding clips to your project, let me plant a bug in your ear: You're going to want to start fine-tuning every clip you add, but you should resist that impulse. In my experience, it's best to throw together a rough assembly of clips to get a big-picture sense of what the movie is going to be, and *then* go back and edit them down in a second pass. It's tough—well, it's tough for me—because editing is the most fun part of building a movie, but it's too easy to get hung up on tiny, time-consuming edits at the start.

Add clips to the project

iMovie offers a few methods for adding footage to your project, all of which are designed to populate your project quickly. If the Show Advanced Tools option is enabled, there's an even faster way to do it.

Adding clips

1. In the Event browser, click and drag to select a range of footage within a clip (**Figure 2.15**). Or, click once to select a 4-second range. To quickly select an entire clip, hold the Command key and click once on the clip.

Figure 2.15
Dragging left to right to select a range of frames within a clip.

2. Do one of the following to add the selection to your movie:

   - Click the Add Selected Video to Project button in the toolbar. The clip appears at the end of your project.

   - Press the E key, which also adds the clip to the end of your project.

   - Drag the selected area to the project (**Figure 2.16**). Make sure you drop it at the end of the project, or between any existing clips; dropping a clip onto another clip leads to more options (detailed in Chapter 4).

Figure 2.16
Drag a clip selection to the Project browser to add it to your movie.

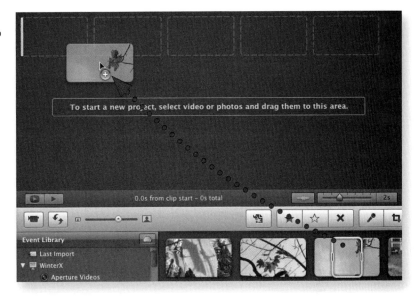

Adding clips using the advanced tools

With iMovie's advanced tools enabled, the Add Selected Video to Project button becomes the Edit tool. Initially it looks and acts the same as when the advanced tools are off, but instead of being a one-click action button, it's now a selectable tool.

1. Click the Edit tool button in the toolbar. The mouse pointer includes a small version of the button's icon.

2. Drag over a selection of video you want to add to the project (or click once to grab a 4-second range) (**Figure 2.17**). The footage is *immediately* added to your movie when you release the mouse button. Also, the tool remains active, so you can drag over other clips to add their frames quickly.

Figure 2.17
Dragging with the Edit tool immediately adds the clip to the project.

3. Click the Edit tool button again, or click the Arrow tool, to exit the Edit tool mode. (You can also press Esc or Return.)

Rearrange clips

A great advantage of video editing is that you can arrange clips however you wish—nothing needs to be chronological. With a project now full of clips, feel free to move their order.

Rearranging clips

1. In the Project browser, click a clip to select it.

2. Drag the clip to the space between two other clips where you want it to appear; a solid green line tells you where the clip will end up when you release the mouse button (**Figure 2.18**).

 You can't drag just a portion of a clip to another location in your project; to do that, it must first be split.

Figure 2.18
Rearranging a clip.

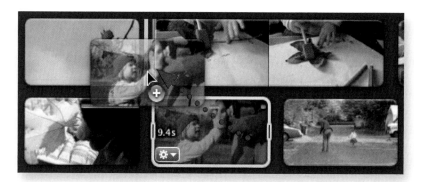

Create a Movie Trailer

Now that you understand the basics of adding clips, I want to take a little side trip into one of the most fun features of iMovie '11: movie trailers. With a minimal amount of work, you can turn your footage into a professionally edited teaser, complete with a soundtrack recorded by the London Symphony Orchestra. It's a fast, fun way to share a few minutes of video without taking the time to edit a movie from start to finish.

Choose a trailer style

Looking for a fast-paced action trailer or something more mysterious? You'll likely find something interesting among iMovie's 15 trailer styles.

Creating a movie trailer

1. Choose File > New Project (or press Command-N).

2. In the New Project dialog, click a movie trailer icon to view a preview (**Figure 2.19**).

Figure 2.19
Previewing a movie trailer style.

> **tip**
>
> **The preview comes up automatically, but you don't need to watch it every time. Click the preview area to pause playback of the sample.**

Below the preview area, each trailer indicates how many "cast members" (that's Hollywood-speak for "people," although in the case of the Pets theme, it can include animals, too) the theme is designed to accommodate.

3. When you've decided on a trailer style, enter a title in the Name field.

4. Choose a frame size from the Aspect Ratio pop-up menu. Unlike regular projects, which adapt the aspect ratio based on the first clip you add, movie trailers crop the clips to fit. So, for example, adding a standard 4:3 clip to a widescreen trailer cuts the top and bottom edges from the image to fit the full width of the frame.

5. Click the Create button to create the trailer.

Edit titles and add clips to the trailer

Most of the editing work is already done for each trailer: clips are timed to match the background music. Your job is to edit the text that appears and choose which video clips to use for each scene.

Adding content to the trailer

1. In the Outline tab, scroll down and replace any of the text with your own. For example, clicking the Movie Name field reveals separate fields for each styled section of text (**Figure 2.20**).

    Some fields also include pop-up menus to access related options, such as whether a cast member is male or female, or to choose the logo style used for the Studio section.

Figure 2.20
Edit the text placeholders.

2. Click the Storyboard tab. Each edit is represented by a thumbnail image containing a placeholder animatic that indicates what type of clip would work best in that spot. The first thumbnail is selected.

3. Drag across a clip in the Event browser to add it to the trailer (**Figure 2.21**). (You'll notice this is the same behavior as the Edit tool when Show Advanced Tools is enabled, described earlier.) iMovie automatically selects the next placeholder.

Figure 2.21
Dragging over a clip adds the footage to a selected placeholder.

You don't have to be precise when selecting a range of footage to include in a clip. No matter how much video you drag, the clip in the trailer remains at a fixed length. You'll be able to fine-tune which portion appears in each scene later.

4. Continue populating the clips with footage from your library. Don't worry if the clips' content doesn't match the suggested animatic.

5. Click the text that appears between scenes and edit it as you see fit.

 6. When you're done adding content, click the Play or Play Full Screen button to watch the trailer.

 If you want to use different footage than what you originally applied to a clip, click the clip to select it and then drag over the new video in the Event browser.

Fine-tuning which section appears in each clip

 1. Click the button in the lower-left corner of a clip to open iMovie's Clip Trimmer.

2. Drag the selection left or right to choose which section of video will appear in the clip (**Figure 2.22**).

3. Click Done to apply the change.

Figure 2.22
The selection area defines the visible part of the video.

 Although the timing of each clip in a trailer is fixed, you can still apply video and audio effects. For example, double-clicking a clip brings up the Clip inspector, where additional transformations are available (I talk about them in greater detail later in the book). To learn about more ways to edit movie trailers, see my Macworld article, "Mastering iMovie trailers," (www.macworld.com/article/156828/2011/01/imovietrailer).

Master Video Editing Basics

The point of editing video is to remove the portions that are bad or middling and keep the portions that are good. That sounds simplistic (and not terribly romantic), but it's through this process that you find a story or a moving document of an event. This section is devoted to the mechanics of trimming footage so only the good portions remain. The more you edit, the more these techniques will become part of your muscle memory, letting you focus on the movie instead of the controls.

Trim in the Project browser

Earlier, I urged you to not try to make every clip perfect when you add it to the Project browser. Now, it's time to pay more attention to the specific frames that make up each clip. There are several techniques to trim footage within your project.

Making and adjusting a selection

1. Just as you did in the Event browser, click and drag within a clip in the Project browser to select a range of frames.

2. Drag the selection handles at the left and right edges to adjust the selection (**Figure 2.23**). As you drag, the selection's duration appears to the right of the selection box.

Figure 2.23
Drag to make a selection.

Action menu   Clip duration   Selection handle   Selection duration

3. If you want to keep the duration of the current selection, but change which frames it exposes, drag the top or bottom edge of the selection box. (This technique is also known as "slipping" a clip.)

> **tip**
>
> **To quickly preview just the selected range of frames in the Viewer, press the forward-slash (/) key.**

Using Trim to Selection

With a selection made, choose Clip > Trim to Selection, or press Command-B. iMovie "crops" the clip so that only the selected area remains in the project. This is the technique I find myself using most of the time, because it lets me specify the section of a clip I want to keep in my movie and removes the rest.

Deleting frames

The opposite of trimming to a selection is to simply delete the highlighted frames by pressing the Delete key.

 As you'll see shortly in "Edit in the Clip Trimmer," deleting footage from a clip in the Project browser doesn't actually delete anything. What you're really doing is choosing which portion of the overall clip (that exists in the Event browser) is visible in your movie. You can get the "deleted" clips back.

Splitting a clip

iMovie gives you two ways to split a clip, which creates an edit break while leaving the clip in the Project browser.

1. First, do one of the following:

    *   Make a selection within the clip.

    *   Position your mouse pointer over the frame you want to split, but do not make a selection.

2. Choose Clip > Split Clip, press Command-Shift-S, or choose Split Clip from the contextual menu (**Figure 2.24**)—the regular menu is unavailable if a selection isn't made, because you'd have to move the mouse pointer to go select the menu item.

Figure 2.24
You can split a clip in one place by using the contextual menu.

If you split at the playhead, you'll see two clips. If you made a selection, you'll see two or three clips, because the split occurs wherever the selection appears (**Figure 2.25**).

Figure 2.25
Splitting a clip.

Selection within a clip

Splitting at the playhead

tip You can recognize a split clip by looking at its corners: If they're sharp, not rounded, the clip has been split. To reunite the segments, select one and then choose Clip > Join Clip, or choose Join Clip from the contextual menu.

Fine-tune trim in place

Quite often, I want to trim just a second or two of footage from a clip. Here's a quick way to do it that I use all the time.

Using fine-tuning controls, the long way

1. Choose iMovie > Preferences and click the Browser button.

2. Enable the Show Fine Tuning Controls button.

3. Click the Fine Tuning button that appears on the clip near the edge where you wish to edit.

4. Drag the handle of the orange selection bar that appears to show or hide individual frames (**Figure 2.26**).

Figure 2.26
The fine-tuning handle
adjusts clips by single
frames.

Using fine-tuning controls, the short way

Go back to iMovie's preferences and disable the Show Fine Tuning
Controls option. Leave it off—you don't need it. Instead, simply hold the
Command and Option keys when your mouse pointer is near a clip's
edge to make the orange selection bar appear.

Edit in the Clip Trimmer

The previous editing techniques happen in the Project browser, but they
all have one shortcoming: You can see only the footage that's visible in
each clip. For a broader perspective of all the video in a clip, edit in the
Clip Trimmer. You can view an entire source clip at once, and see which
section is currently visible within your project.

Editing in the Clip Trimmer

1. Click the Action menu for the clip you want to edit, and choose Clip
   Trimmer (**Figure 2.27**). The Clip Trimmer slides over the Project
   Library and Project browser areas.

Figure 2.27
Opening the
Clip Trimmer

2. Drag the selection handles of the visible area to adjust which part of the clip appears in your project (**Figure 2.28**).

Figure 2.28
View an entire clip in the Clip Trimmer.

3. Click Done to apply the edit and close the Clip Trimmer.

tip

You can edit other clips without closing the Clip Trimmer. Click any clip in the Project browser, or click the left or right button at the top of the Clip Trimmer to switch to the previous or next clip.

Master Audio Editing Basics

iMovie handles audio a bit differently than other editors, which can be especially confusing for people new to the program. Typically, video software includes two or more audio tracks on which songs, sound effects, and other audio are placed (in addition to the audio portion of the video clips). iMovie offers...none. At least, none that are apparent. In reality, you can add as many sounds as your Mac's memory will allow, which is more than you're likely to ever need.

Add a background song

If anything, adding audio is one of the most confusing aspects of iMovie, because the software considers there to be two types of audio: background songs and audio clips. The difference isn't in file formats, but in usage. A background song sits *behind* the video—quite literally, the way iMovie displays it—and doesn't act the way other audio clips do. The approach, I'm sure, attempts to make audio less intimidating for most users, who presumably want to just throw in a song as the movie's soundtrack.

Adding a background song

1. Open the Music and Sound Effects browser by clicking its button in the toolbar (or by pressing Command-1).

2. Click a media source in the top pane of the browser (**Figure 2.29**). iMovie can pull audio from your iTunes library, GarageBand, or select folders on your Mac.

Figure 2.29
Previewing a song in the Music and Sound Effects browser.

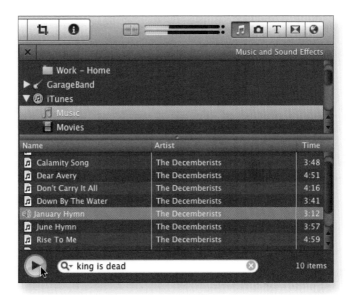

3. Use the search field at the bottom to quickly locate a song if you know its name, artist, or album. Clicking the Play button to the left previews the song.

4. When you've selected a song, drag it to the Project browser. However, pay attention: Make sure you drag to the edge of the window so the background of the browser is *green* (**Figure 2.30**).

Figure 2.30
Adding a background song.

The song appears as a large green field behind the video clips and plays along with the video (**Figure 2.31**).

Figure 2.31
The background song really does appear in the background.

 tip   In the Music and Sound Effects browser, click a column heading to sort the list by that attribute. I often sort by Time when I know I need a song of a certain duration. Click it again to reverse the sort.

Adding multiple background songs

When you add a background song, it automatically starts playing at the beginning of the movie. Adding another song in the same way makes it appear after the first one, so they play back-to-back (**Figure 2.32**).

Figure 2.32
A second background song appears immediately after the first.

Re-ordering background songs

What if you want the second song to appear at the start of the movie? Here is, in my opinion, the oddest feature implementation within iMovie, because it seems so different than everything else.

1. Choose Clip > Arrange Music Tracks.

2. In the dialog that appears, drag the song titles under Floating Music Tracks to change their order of appearance (**Figure 2.33**).

3. Click OK when you're done.

Figure 2.33
Re-ordering a background song so it plays first.

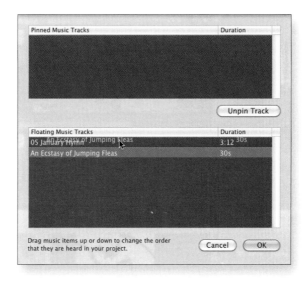

Pinning background songs

It's possible to "pin" a background song to a portion of video so that it stays with that clip. (For example, if you want a song to begin at a certain scene in your movie.) To do so, just drag the song's title to the spot where you want it to appear; the song becomes purple to indicate that it's pinned (**Figure 2.34**).

Figure 2.34
Pinning a clip.

However, there's a caveat: If you add a new background song to the movie, it fills in any gap in background music. So, for example, if you pinned a song so it plays at the beginning of the second clip, and then you add a new song, the new song ends up *ahead of* the pinned clip (**Figure 2.35**).

Figure 2.35
Pinning the first song forced the next song to appear at the beginning.

Once a clip is pinned, you can release it by clicking to select it and then either choosing Clip > Unpin Music Track or choosing the same item from the contextual menu.

To avoid this strange circumstance, I recommend adding songs and other audio files as a regular audio clip, and using the background song for when you need just one or two pieces of audio that will all float or will all be pinned.

Add an audio clip

The other method of adding audio to a project is to drag an audio file from the Music and Sound Effects browser directly onto a video clip in your movie. It appears as a green bar beneath the video thumbnails and is locked to the clip where you dropped it (**Figure 2.36**).

Figure 2.36
Drag an audio clip to your project (left), where it attaches to a video clip (right).

You can reposition the audio clip by dragging it to a new location within the browser. To change the clip's duration, drag its left or right edge.

> iMovie supports nearly unlimited layered audio clips, although that's not obvious because there are no visible audio tracks as you'd find in other video editors. When you drag an additional clip to an area where there's an existing audio clip, the new one is stacked along with it (Figure 2.37). This is a great way to layer multiple sound effects as well as music and dialog clips.

Figure 2.37
You want multiple audio tracks? Just keep adding clips.

Change clip volume

If everything in a movie were blasting at the same volume level, it would be difficult to separate music from dialogue, sound effects from ambient noise. In iMovie, the volume levels can be changed in a number of ways.

Changing volume using audio waveforms

1. Click the Show Audio Waveforms button in the browser to display a visual representation of the audio below each clip (or, in the case of audio-only clips, below the clip's title).

2. The black horizontal line, the volume bar, represents the clip's volume level; drag it down to decrease the volume, or up to increase (**Figure 2.38**). The waveforms adjust to indicate the change.

Figure 2.38
Changing the clip's overall volume level.

Changing volume using the Audio Adjustments inspector

1. Double-click a clip to bring up the Clip inspector and then click the Audio button; or, choose Audio Adjustments from the Action menu. You can also select a clip and press the A key.

2. Drag the Volume slider left or right to adjust the level (**Figure 2.39**).

Figure 2.39
Changing volume in the Audio Adjustments inspector.

Fade audio in or out

A frequently used technique for polishing audio is to fade the volume up at the beginning of a clip, or down at the end. As with changing the overall volume of a clip, there are two ways of applying audio fades.

Fading audio using waveforms

1. In the Project browser, locate the fade handles at the edges of a clip's waveform display.

2. Drag the fade handle to set the point at which the clip arrives at full volume (**Figure 2.40**).

Figure 2.40
Adjusting the fade-in of a clip's audio.

Fade-in   Fade-out

Fading audio using the Audio Adjustments inspector

1. Bring up the Audio Adjustments inspector.

2. Drag the Fade In or Fade Out sliders to adjust the fade (**Figure 2.41**).

Figure 2.41
Fade controls in the
Audio Adjustments
inspector.

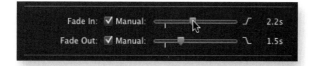

Adjust volume within a clip

Until iMovie '11, that was about the extent of how you could edit audio
clips (aside from applying audio effects, which I describe elsewhere in
the book). But what if a loud noise, like a background sneeze, interrupts
a scene? When you want to change the volume on just a portion of a
clip's audio, do the following.

Adjusting volume within a clip

1. Make sure the audio waveforms are visible.

2. Click within the waveform area and drag to select a portion of the
    audio you wish to edit (**Figure 2.42**).

3. Drag the volume bar within the selection. Notice that iMovie auto-
    matically applies a transition so the volume doesn't change suddenly.

Figure 2.42
Lowering the volume
of a portion of a clip.

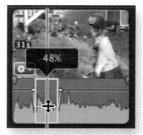

4. Drag one of the yellow dots that appeared on the volume bar to
    adjust the duration of the transition.

**To quickly mute a section of audio, select it and press the Delete key.
Pressing the key again restores the volume to its previous level. If you
want to mute an entire clip, select it and either choose Clip > Mute Clip
or press Command-Shift-M.**

Add Titles

We've come a long way since the days when the only text you could add to your video was the date and time permanently burned into one corner of the image by your camcorder. iMovie's titles feature professional typography, eye-catching animation, and the capability to refine typographic elements.

Add a title

A title appears in your project like any other clip, but it is positioned above the clip thumbnails and colored blue to differentiate it from the other types of clips.

Adding a title

1. Open the Title browser by clicking its button in the toolbar or by pressing Command-3.

2. Choose a title style you want to use. Holding your mouse pointer over a title animates the thumbnail to give you a preview of its effect (**Figure 2.43**).

Figure 2.43
Preview the available title styles by hovering over them.

3. Drag the title thumbnail to the location in your project where you want the title to appear.

When you move the title to a video clip, a portion of the clip high-lights in blue (**Figure 2.44**). This identifies the title's duration, and can be at the beginning, at the end, or over the entire clip.

Figure 2.44
Adding a title to the first part of a clip.

Title previously placed

4. Release the mouse button to add the title.

 Holding the Shift key before you drop the title highlights a four-second block of footage, versus the start, end, or entirety of the clip. This option gives you more control over where the title appears—you can adjust the duration after you've added the title.

Editing the text

1. In the Viewer, replace the "Title Text Here" wording with your own text (**Figure 2.45**).

Figure 2.45
Type your own text.

2. Click the Preview button in the Viewer to see how the title animates, or scrub the playhead over the clip in the Project browser.

3. Click Done to finish editing the text.

Changing the title style

To try a different title appearance, drag a thumbnail from the Title browser and drop it onto the video clip where the existing title resides (make sure you see the blue highlight; dropping onto the title clip itself does nothing, something I must frequently remind myself when I'm trying to change styles). iMovie keeps your text and applies the new format.

If you've placed more than one title in your project, dragging a new style to an existing title gives you the option of replacing the style (but not the text) of just that title or all titles (**Figure 2.46**).

Figure 2.46
Changing a title style gives you the option of changing all titles in the project.

 The Four Corners title has a hidden surprise: If you repeat the title style back-to-back, the text appears from different corners and in different colors for up to four instances (one for each corner).

Customize the text appearance

The built-in styles are slick, but I know you're itching to personalize their appearance. With all of the fonts available on your Mac, it would be a crime to not even experiment a little. Two methods are available: You can choose a new typeface, color, and size using the iMovie Font panel; or, you can broaden the typographic possibilities by switching to the System Font panel.

Some titles, such as Boogie Lights and Pixie Dust, do not allow changes to the formatting.

Customizing the text appearance with the iMovie Font panel

1. Select a title in your project.

2. In the Viewer, click the Show Fonts button to bring up the iMovie Font panel.

3. Move the mouse pointer over a font name to preview the title in that typeface (**Figure 2.47**); skimming the row lets you see the appearance of the entire title animation.

Figure 2.47
Choose from a collection of fonts, colors, and sizes.

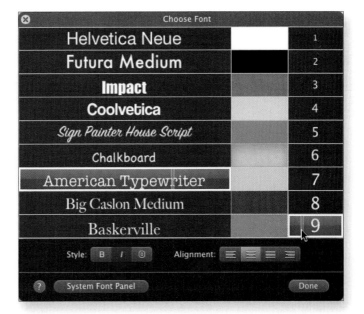

4. Click a typeface name to select it and lock in that font for the title.

5. Hover over the font color and font size columns to preview how they affect the text, clicking the ones you wish to apply. Note that the font sizes apply to all text in the title, so smaller-sized subtitles will become the same size as the main title.

6. Choose a style (bold, italic, outline, or any combination of the three) by clicking one of the Style buttons.

7. Click one of the Alignment buttons if you want to change where the text lines up relative to the Viewer window: flush left, centered, justified, or flush right.

8. Click Done to apply the style changes.

In iMovie's preferences, you can edit the options that appear in the iMovie Font panel. For example, suppose you need a piece of identifying text to appear in the corner of every movie your company creates. Choose iMovie > Preferences and click the Fonts button. Click the name of a font to access all installed fonts from a pop-up menu and choose one. For colors, click a color swatch and then, in the system Colors panel that appears, choose a new color. You can also change the Opacity setting here, to make text that's mostly translucent and less obtrusive.

Customizing the text appearance using the System Font panel

1. Select a title in the Project browser.

2. Select the range of text you want to edit. This step is important; otherwise, iMovie doesn't know on which text to apply new formatting.

3. Click the System Font Panel button at the bottom of the window. The panel flips around to reveal the expanded typographic options available from Mac OS X (**Figure 2.48**).

Figure 2.48
Choose from a collection of fonts, colors, and sizes.

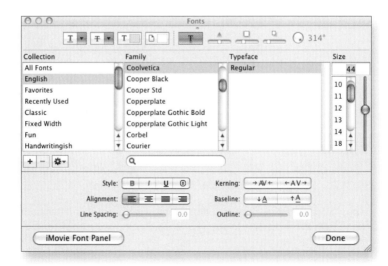

4. Using the controls in this panel, choose from all fonts installed on your computer, and edit attributes such as text shadow, kerning, and underlining. The Action menu below the Collection column leads to even more controls, such as an easy way to locate custom characters and additional typographic options (like ligatures and "old-style" numbers) for fonts that support them.

   To edit a different block of text in your title, you can just select that text; you don't need to close the System Font panel first.

5. When you're finished editing, click Done.

   The next time you click the Show Fonts button in the Viewer, you'll see the System Font panel; click the iMovie Font Panel button to switch back to iMovie's implementation.

Add Transitions

We've been exposed to video our entire lives, so our brains have no trouble following a sequence of many clips that are cut back-to-back. But sometimes you want a transition that bridges two clips in a stylistic way, whether to express a mood or add visual interest. iMovie's themes also make extensive use of transitions; I cover them in "Customize a Theme Project" in Chapter 4.

Add a transition

A transition sits between two clips and merges them together in an interesting way. My preference is to keep things simple: A Cross Dissolve does the job without attracting too much attention, although the Swap transition is fun and flashy when the movie calls for that.

Adding a transition

1. Open the Transition browser by clicking its button in the toolbar (or by pressing Command-4).

2. Choose a transition to use; holding your mouse pointer over a transition's thumbnail offers a preview of the effect.

3. Drag a transition from the Transition browser to the space between two clips in your project. The transition appears as a small icon in the gap (**Figure 2.49**).

Figure 2.49
A transition placed between two clips.

Moving or deleting a transition

You can drag a transition to any space between clips in your project and keep its settings. To remove a transition, click to select it and then press the Delete key.

Edit transition settings

Unlike in most video editors, adding a transition in iMovie doesn't require that the interim footage be rendered to disk as a mini-clip of its own. That means you can quickly adjust a transition's duration and style without waiting for clips to re-render.

Changing the transition style

1. Double-click a transition to bring up the Transition inspector. You can also choose Transition Adjustments from the Action menu that appears below the transition's icon.

2. In the inspector, click the Transition pop-up menu, which flips over to reveal all of the transition styles (**Figure 2.50**).

Figure 2.50
iMovie includes a live preview of your clips in each thumbnail.

3. Click a transition to choose it.

4. Click Done to exit the inspector.

 Another option is to drag a style from the Transition browser onto the transition in your project you want to change. That gives you the additional option of replacing all transitions in your movie with that style.

Changing the transition duration

1. Double-click a transition to bring up the Transition inspector.

2. Enter a time in the Duration field (**Figure 2.51**).

   If you want to set every transition in the project to the same duration, enable the "Applies to all transitions" checkbox.

Figure 2.51
Changing the duration in the Transition inspector.

3. Click Done to exit the Inspector.

 The default duration of a transition is 0.5 seconds, but you can change that. Choose File > Project Properties and adjust the Transition Duration slider. To alter the timing of all transitions in your project, enable the Applies to All Transitions button; to keep existing transitions' durations and set the timing to new transitions, enable the Applies When Adding to Project button.

 A transition's duration depends on how much footage is available in each of the surrounding clips. If you want a 5-second transition, but the clip to the left is only 2 seconds in duration, iMovie makes the clip 0.9 seconds (leaving 1 second of the clip visible before the transition) and displays the time above the transition icon in yellow.

Apply One-Step Effects

iMovie '11 added a new feature that lets you apply a few common editing effects with one menu selection that would normally require several steps. The One-Step Effects feature can make footage play in slow motion or sped up, create an instant replay, and more. By way of example, I'll apply an instant replay to a portion of a clip.

Creating an instant replay effect

1. Select a range of footage in your movie that you'd like to be replayed (**Figure 2.52**).

Figure 2.52
Make a selection to use for the effect.

2. Choose Clip > Instant Replay and choose a speed (50%, 25%, or 10%) for the slow-motion portion of the effect.

   iMovie splits the clip, makes a copy of the selected video, adjusts its speed, and adds a custom "Instant Replay" title to the section (**Figure 2.53**).

Figure 2.53
Instant replay applied.

tip Although multiple steps were required to achieve the effect, you can go back to the previous state by choosing Edit > Undo or by pressing Command-Z. Also, the edits are entirely editable. So, for example, if you want to change the style of the title, or adjust the speed of the slow-motion clip, you can do that manually.

3

Organize Your
Video Library

I'm sure you're itching to start editing in earnest, and by all means jump
to the projects ahead if you can't wait. But hear me out before you leap.
Although organizing one's video library sounds like cleaning your room
or making sense of your desk, putting a little time into managing your
iMovie library pays dividends later.

A serious challenge in video editing is locating good footage to use. It's
there in your library—you shot it, you know it's there—hidden among hours
of other video. iMovie includes tools to mark good sections, hide clips
you'll never use in a project, and locate people who appear in the scenes.
You can also assign keywords to footage, making it possible to display only
those clips marked, for example, with a favorite city or person.

This chapter also tackles some basic, but important, video-management
tasks such as moving Events to an external hard disk when your Mac's
internal drive fills up, and merging and splitting Events.

Organize Events Project

Difficulty level: Easy

Each time you import footage into iMovie, you're given the option of creating a new Event or adding the clips to an existing Event. But there may come a point where you want to reorganize your library. Perhaps, for example, you'd rather break an Event for one long vacation into separate Events for each destination.

Another common need is to move old video to an external hard drive to make room for new footage. When I bought a MacBook Pro last year, I figured its 500 GB hard disk would give me plenty of breathing room, but the space fills up quickly with video and digital photos. This situation becomes even more important if you own a MacBook Air or other Mac with a comparatively limited amount of storage.

Rename, merge, or split Events

The point of the Event Library is to make it easier to locate your footage, but that's difficult when the library is made up of numerous Events with titles such as "New Event 2-19-11". Instead, take those anonymous entities, rename them, and turn them into Events that make sense so you'll know at a glance which footage will appear when you click an Event.

For example, I often use two cameras (one camera and my iPhone) that to record video, which I import separately into two Events. But the clips are shot at the same gathering, so I'd rather they all appear in one Event.

Or, consider the reverse: Suppose you imported your vacation footage as a single batch of video. You can split the footage into multiple Events and organize the footage by days or locations.

Renaming an Event

1. In the Event Library, double-click an Event name to select it.

2. Type a new name, and press Return.

Merging Events

1. In the Event Library, select the Events you wish to merge into one.

2. Choose File > Merge Events, or choose Merge Events from the contextual menu (**Figure 3.1**).

3. In the dialog that appears, enter a name for the new Event.

  A faster method of merging Events is to select one or more and then drag them onto another Event.

Figure 3.1
Merging Events using
the contextual menu

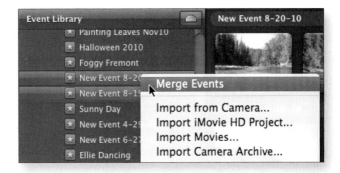

Splitting an Event

1. In the Event Library, select the Event you wish to break up.

2. In the Event browser, locate the clip *after* the one you wish to include in a new Event (**Figure 3.2**).

Figure 3.2
Preparing to split
an Event

Clips to split into new Event

3. Control-click the clip to select it in its entirety.

4. Choose File > Split Event Before Selected Clip. iMovie creates a new Event with the same name as the original clip, appended with a version number (such as "Mount Rainier Vacation 1").

5. Rename the Events to make them easier to identify (**Figure 3.3**).

Figure 3.3
I've split the Event into two new ones and renamed them.

 You can also select clips in one Event and drag them to another Event to reorganize them.

Creating new Events

If you want to be proactive about managing your footage, you can create new empty Events. Then, when you're importing new clips, your organization scheme is already in place and you don't have to come up with it on the fly. Choose File > New Event, which adds an Event with today's date.

 Another reason to create a new Event is to consolidate video footage that may be stored in iPhoto or Aperture. Sure, the clips are available by clicking the iPhoto or Aperture name in the Event sidebar, but when one is selected you see all the video stored in that library. Instead, consider creating a new Event and dragging the clips from the photo library to your Event Library. The clips are copied, so they'll exist in two places on your hard disk (the photo library and the iMovie library), but having them in an iMovie Event may make it easier to locate the ones you want to use.

Move or copy Events to a different hard disk

You may be tempted to move your library's video files yourself in the Finder; they're easy to find in the Movies folder in your Home folder. Don't do it! It's much better to let iMovie handle the heavy lifting, because it can then better keep track of where everything is. Don't worry, it's actually easier to accomplish within the application than in the Finder.

Moving or copying an Event

1. First, make sure you can view other volumes by choosing View > Group Events By Disk, or by clicking the hard disk icon in the upper-right corner of the Event Library.

2. Drag an Event from your internal hard disk to the name of the other disk, but keep the following in mind as you do so:

   - To *copy* the Event, just drag it to the destination. The mouse pointer includes a green + icon to indicate that a copy will be made (**Figure 3.4**).

   - To *move* the Event, which *deletes the footage* from the original location after the files have been copied, hold the Command key while dragging.

   The files are copied or moved to the destination disk.

Figure 3.4
Copying an Event to an external disk

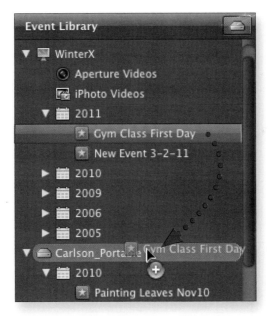

> **tip** You can also drag an Event onto the name of another Event on the destination drive to add the footage into one Event. You'll be asked to enter a name for the merged Event.

Copy or move projects (and related footage) to a different hard disk

You may wish to move a project, not just an Event, to another hard disk, either for archiving or for transfer between a desktop computer and a laptop. Be sure you have the Group Events By Project option enabled to view the drives.

Copying or moving a project

1. In the Project Library, drag a project to another drive. As with Events, the default action is to copy the project, but if you hold the Command key as you drag, iMovie will move the project, deleting the original.

2. In the dialog that appears, choose whether to copy only the project file, or the project file and the Events that include footage used in the project (**Figure 3.5**).

Figure 3.5
Copying a project also gives you the option to copy associated Events.

Some clips used in the project are not on the hard disk "Carlson_Portable." To consolidate all clips onto your hard disk, do one of the following:

Copy project (120 MB)

Copy project and Events (136 MB)

Cancel

note If you copy an edited project back to the source location, iMovie does not overwrite the original version. Instead, the project appears in addition to the original, with a version number appended (such as "My Project 1").

Mark Favorite Videos Project

Difficulty level: Easy

In my imagination, I'm a superb videographer who captures only the best moments. In reality, I'm quite typical in that a lot of footage ends up either *just fine* or completely unusable. With a lot of video stored in your iMovie library, how do you find the good stuff? The secret is to highlight favorite sections so you can easily locate them later, and to hide rejected sections that you know will never make it into a movie.

Mark favorites

Although iMovie's live-preview filmstrips make it possible to see what a clip has to offer, sometimes the good sections might not be immediately apparent, such as when the clips size slider is set to reveal thumbnails for every 30 seconds of footage. Spend some time marking favorites, and then display only those good clips when you build your project.

Marking favorite footage

1. Select a range of frames you want to highlight as a favorite.

2. Click the Mark Selected Video as Favorite button, or press the F key (**Figure 3.6**). iMovie adds a green bar to indicate the section has been marked.

   With Show Advanced Tools enabled in iMovie's preferences, you can first click the Favorite tool (the tool's name when nothing is selected) and then drag across ranges of video to mark them.

3. Continue to mark favorites until you've tagged all the good sections.

Figure 3.6
Marking a section as a favorite

Section to be marked favorite   *Favorite indicator*

Removing the favorite marks

Did you get too favorite-happy? Select a range of footage and click the Unmark Selected Video button (or press the U key). Or, click the Unmark tool and drag it over footage to remove the mark.

Viewing only favorite clips

When you're ready to start adding clips to your project, choose Favorites Only from the Show pop-up menu (**Figure 3.7**). Footage not marked is hidden, leaving only the good footage visible.

Figure 3.7
Show favorites only.

Hide rejected clips

What about those clips that are never going to appear in a movie? Those minutes when you didn't think the camera was recording, or maybe the focus was off? Mark them as rejected to hide them from view, and optionally throw them in the Trash.

Rejecting clips

1. Select a range of frames you want to reject.

2. Click the Mark Selected Video as Rejected button, or press the R key. The section is immediately hidden.

   (With the advanced tools enabled, you can also click the Reject tool and drag across footage you wish to remove.)

tip   Highlighting a range of video and pressing the Delete key also marks that footage as rejected.

Viewing rejected clips

From the Show pop-up menu, choose either All Clips, which reveals rejected footage marked with a red line, or Rejected Only, which shows only clips marked for rejection.

If you want to remove the rejected label from a clip, select it and click the Unmark Selected Clip button in the toolbar.

Moving rejected clips to the Trash

The benefit to hiding rejected clips is that they're still available in case you change your mind. (You may want a soft-focus version of a scene, for example.) However, if you really don't want the rejected footage cluttering up your hard disk, choose Rejected Only from the Show pop-up menu and then click the Move Rejected to Trash button (**Figure 3.8**).

Figure 3.8
Rejected clips, bound for the digital dustbin

Doing so requires a bit of work on iMovie's part. For rejected footage that's part of a longer clip, iMovie rewrites the video file on disk so it no longer includes the rejected section; that could result in one clip being split into multiple clips, in the case of rejected footage that appears in the middle of a clip. The original clip is then moved to the Trash in the Finder. To really delete the footage from your hard disk, choose Finder > Empty Trash.

> **tip**
>
> **To go a step further, consider running iMovie's Space Saver feature. When you choose File > Space Saver, you have the option of sending to the Trash entire clips that include rejected footage but are unused in any project, are not marked as a favorite, or don't include keywords.**

Find people in your videos

Another way to cut down on the time you spend scanning footage is to let iMovie help you find scenes where people are present. Using face-detection technology, iMovie can mark scenes where people—or things that resemble people—appear. Note that this feature only detects people; it doesn't identify them. (But keep reading this chapter to learn a technique to mark who appears in your video.)

Finding people in footage

1. Select an Event, or a clip within an Event or in a project.

2. Choose File > Analyze Video and choose a submenu: Stabilization and People, or just People. Choosing the latter results in less time spent analyzing the footage.

3. When iMovie is finished, video containing people is marked with a purple link (**Figure 3.9**).

Figure 3.9
The purple line indicates that people are present.

View only footage that contains people

Viewing only footage marked with people

Click the People button next to the Show pop-up menu to hide footage that does not contain people.

 iMovie looks for faces when searching for people, so although you may have some footage that clearly includes people (as in the figure above), the software doesn't mark the sections unless faces are easily detected.

 The People feature also looks for other people-related characteristics, such as whether there are two people in a scene, or if the shot is a closeup. These are assigned keyword tags, which I get into next.

Tag Your Videos Project

Difficulty level: Intermediate

iMovie offers one more powerful way to organize your video library, which I suspect many people overlook: You can assign keyword tags to footage to make it easier to locate footage that shares similar attributes. For example, perhaps you want to reveal all video that was shot outdoors, or all video containing a favorite pet. When you're looking for the perfect sunset to cap off the end of a video, a couple of clicks can bring up all of your best late-afternoon footage.

Keywording is a feature that appears only when you enable Show Advanced Tools in iMovie's preferences, so make sure that option is turned on.

Apply keyword tags

iMovie includes several general-purpose keywords to get you started, but you can also create your own. Two modes let you apply tags by dragging across footage (similar to the way the marking tools work) or by first selecting footage and then choosing which tags to use.

Applying keyword tags using the Auto-Apply mode

1. Click the Keyword tool (or press K) to display the Keywords panel (**Figure 3.10**).

Figure 3.10
The Keywords panel

2. Click the checkboxes for any keywords you wish to apply. When multiple terms are checked, any footage you tag receives all of them.

   To add your own keyword, type it in the New Keyword field and click the Add button. (Similarly, selecting a keyword and clicking the Remove button deletes the term from the list. If you've previously applied the term to other footage, removing the keyword from the list also removes it from the footage.)

3. Drag across the footage you wish to tag with the active keywords (**Figure 3.11**). A blue line appears to indicate keywords are applied.

Figure 3.11
Applying keywords

tip A quick way to see which tags have been applied to a range of video is to turn on the Playhead Info display. Choose View > Playhead Info, or press Command-Y.

Applying keyword tags using the Inspector mode

1. Bring up the Keywords panel and click the Inspector button.

2. Select a range of video.

3. Click the checkboxes for the keywords you want to apply.

tip For faster application of keyword tags, select some video and press the number key associated with the term you want (limited to the first nine). You can reorder the items in the list by dragging them.

Use keyword tags to locate footage

With your video tagged, apply filters to view just the clips that match the keywords you choose.

Filtering footage using keyword tags

1. Click the Show or Hide Keyword Filter Pane button to view the pane.

2. To include a keyword in the filter, click the right-hand (green) portion of the lozenge button near that term.

    Clicking the left-hand (red) portion of the lozenge button excludes a term. For example, you could display all clips except those tagged with "Family" by excluding that term.

3. The default filtering approach is to match any term you've chosen. So, selecting "Two People" and "Family" in that case brings up footage that contains *either* term. You can limit the search by clicking the Match: All button, which would display clips that contain both terms (**Figure 3.12**).

Figure 3.12
In this example, the only clips shown are those tagged with "Two People" *and* "Family," and *not* tagged with "Medium."

Show or Hide Keyword Filter Pane button

tip **To temporarily view all footage without losing your filter selections, click the Filter by Keyword checkbox.**

Use tags to identify people

I mentioned that iMovie's People feature only detects people and doesn't identify them. However, if you combine the analysis with keywords, you can mark footage and tag it with specific names. Then, when you're building your movie, you can easily locate video with people you know.

Using tags to identify people

1. Select an Event or some clips and analyze the footage for people (by choosing File > Analyze Video > People).

2. Click the People button next to the Show pop-up menu so you view only footage containing people.

3. Click the Keyword tool (or press K) to bring up the Keywords panel.

4. Type a person's name into the New Keyword field and either press Return or click the Add button.

5. With the Keywords panel in Auto-Apply mode, drag to select sections of the video containing that person (**Figure 3.13**).

6. Repeat the previous two steps for any other people you want to tag.

Figure 3.13
Tagging footage with the name of a specific person

note

When iMovie analyzes footage for people, you'll see several related tags appear, such as One Person, Two People, Group, and Closeup. These tags are especially helpful when you're creating iMovie trailers, which specify those characteristics in some scenes.

4

iMovie Beyond the Basics

Using the techniques covered so far, you can make all kinds of great videos in iMovie. Having a firm grasp of the basics helps you edit projects faster, so you're spending more time enjoying your content and less time feeling your way through the software. But you're bound to run into special situations: What to do when you want to fine-tune the way a transition works between two clips? What if your footage suffers from unexpected camera shake, or if the audio is muddled?

iMovie includes many tools for dealing with special situations, as well as for improving what you've already shot. For example, the color correction controls can boost saturation, adjust white balance, and apply eye-catching video effects. In this chapter, I also dig into advanced editing techniques and building photo slideshows.

Learn Advanced Editing Techniques Project

Difficulty level: Intermediate

Editing video is a process of repeating a few movements—placing, trimming, adjusting—hundreds or thousands of times. So, you won't be surprised that iMovie offers shortcuts to make the work easier. The techniques described here are ones you can use in any movie project, and they focus on inserting clips and replacing existing clips with new ones. I also go into detail about the Precision Editor, a great way of making fine adjustments to the edit points of your clips, and about extracting audio from video clips, a valuable but often overlooked capability.

Insert a clip into the middle of another clip

In Chapter 2, I explained how to split a clip, a technique often used to drop a new clip into the space between the two segments. An easier method is to use iMovie's Insert function.

Inserting a clip

1. In the Event browser, select a section of video you want to add to your project.

2. Drag the clip to the Project browser and drop it onto an existing clip (**Figure 4.1**).

Figure 4.1
Drag a clip to
be inserted.

3. From the pop-up menu that appears, choose Insert (**Figure 4.2**).

Figure 4.2
Choose an action.

The clip in the Project browser is split, and the new clip appears where you dropped it (**Figure 4.3**).

Figure 4.3
The inserted clip

> **tip** When you insert a clip, the next portion of the clip that got split continues where the first portion left off. If you're looking to insert a clip but not interrupt the scene (for example, you want the audio from the first clip to continue while the inserted clip is visible), use a cutaway. See "Create a Cutaway Project," later in this chapter.

Replace clips

I recommend assembling a movie fairly quickly, and then spending time later fine-tuning it. Often, you find that a clip you added isn't as good as another one that would fit in the same place. Instead of deleting the clip and adding the new one, use the Replace commands. This option is particularly helpful when the incoming clip must remain the same dura-tion as the one it's replacing.

Replacing clips

1. Drag a clip from the Event browser onto the top of the clip you want to replace in the Project browser.

2. From the pop-up menu that appears, choose one of the following (**Figure 4.4**):

- **Replace.** The incoming clip completely replaces the clip onto which it was dropped.

- **Replace from Start.** The first frame of your selection becomes the start of the replaced clip (just as the regular Replace function works). However, the duration of the clip remains the same as the clip you're replacing.

  So, for example, if you want to replace a 10-second clip in your project with a 5-second clip from an Event, choosing Replace from Start results in a 10-second clip. iMovie grabs 5 seconds outside your selection to fill the gap.

- **Replace from End.** Similar to the previous option, Replace from End uses the last frame of your selection as the anchor point when replacing a clip. In the example above, 5 seconds of additional footage are pulled from before the selection to maintain the original clip's 10-second duration.

- **Replace at Playhead.** The first frame of your selection appears wherever you position the playhead and release the mouse button. In this case, using the example above, iMovie may grab footage from before or after the selection to fit within the 10-second gap.

 Remember, you can always open the replaced clip in the Clip Trimmer and adjust the visible portion of the footage without changing the duration: Click and drag in the middle of the selection to "slip" the clip.

 If there isn't enough available footage to perform a replace action, iMovie warns you that the edit will shorten the duration of the movie. In my example, if I were to select the first 4 seconds of the clip and drop it into the project using the Replace from End option, iMovie wouldn't have enough source footage to fill the 10-second gap from the end.

Figure 4.4
I'm replacing a 10-second clip in the project (top) with a 5-second selection from the Event browser.

To make it easier to see which footage is used with each Replace command, I've made the replacement and then opened the new project clip in the Clip Trimmer (below, with visible footage selected in yellow). In each case, the same 5-second selection was dragged to the original clip in the movie.

Original clip in project (10 seconds)

Active portion of clip using Replace (5 seconds)

Active portion of clip using Replace from Start

Active portion of clip using Replace from End

Active portion of clip using Replace at Playhead

Edit with the Precision Editor

Moving selection handles in the Project browser is a quick way to edit a clip, but it's not always as precise as you'd like. The Precision Editor, like the Clip Trimmer, is another interface for editing clips, but in this case you get to manipulate the point where two clips meet (including a transition if present), which is referred to as the *cut point*. Having this control is great for fine-tuning not just how a clip ends, but how it interacts with the next clip in the movie.

The Precision Editor looks simple, but there are several ways to edit the elements surrounding a cut point. You can see exactly where two clips overlap, adjust the duration of a transition, and even offset a video clip's audio without extracting it as a separate clip (a technique I discuss a few pages ahead).

To open the Precision Editor, do one of the following:

* Click the Action button on any clip and choose Precision Editor from the menu (**Figure 4.5**).

Figure 4.5
The Precision Editor
pop-up menu item

* If a transition appears between two clips, choose Precision Editor from the Action button that appears below the transition icon when you move your mouse pointer over it.

* Select a clip and press Command-/ (forward slash).

* For a faster, easier method, double-click the space between two clips; or, if a transition is present, double-click the space above the transition icon.

Editing video at a cut point

The Precision Editor displays the clips on either side of a cut point on two levels: the previous clip above and the next clip after (**Figure 4.6**). Visible footage appears in full color, while the hidden portion of a clip is dimmed.

Figure 4.6
The Precision Editor

Previous clip   *Hidden footage*

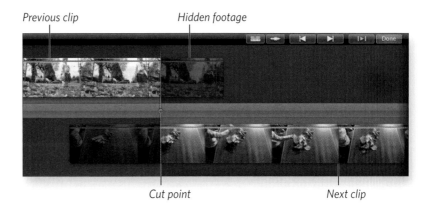

Cut point   *Next clip*

To adjust the cut point, use any of the following methods:

- Drag the center of the cut point left or right. This edit changes the duration of each clip but retains the duration of the overall project (**Figure 4.7**).

Figure 4.7
Adjusting the cut point

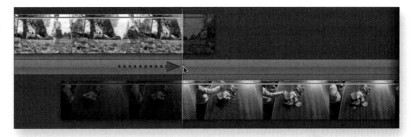

- Drag one of the clips left or right to reposition the cut point of just that clip. For example, dragging the top clip in the figure above would adjust where the clip ends. This technique changes the duration of the project, because you're adding or removing frames from the clip.

- Click once on a clip to set that frame as the cut point. This is often a faster method than dragging the clip.

- Drag the cut point for just one clip (**Figure 4.8**). Doing so doesn't change the cut point in the other clip.

Figure 4.8
Adjusting the cut point
for just one clip

To quickly preview how the edit looks, click the Play Current Edit button. iMovie plays three seconds of footage around the edit point.

tip **Give yourself more room to work in the Precision Editor by minimizing the size of the Viewer. Choose Window > Viewer > Small, or press Command-8.**

Adjusting the duration of a transition

Transitions appear on the middle bar in the Precision Editor and give you a good visual idea of which footage is being used to combine clips. You can also change the duration of a transition by dragging one of its side handles; the time appears as you drag (**Figure 4.9**).

Figure 4.9
Changing the duration of a transition

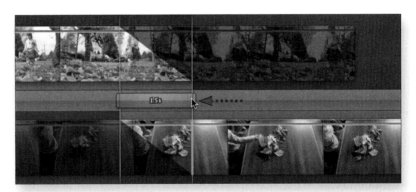

tip **You can change the transition style without opening the Transitions browser by double-clicking the transition in the Precision Editor to bring up the inspector. Then, click the Transition pop-up menu and choose a new style.**

Offsetting an audio transition

One effective way to switch scenes is to start playing audio from the next clip before the visuals appear (think of a scene where dialogue from the previous clip bleeds over the visuals of the next clip, for example). Using the Precision Editor, you can change the audio's offset by dragging a special audio cut point handle.

1. Click the Show or Hide Audio Waveforms button to view the clips' waveforms.

2. Drag the cut point within the audio portion left or right; the amount of offset appears at the top of the Precision Editor (**Figure 4.10**).

To offset the audio in both clips—and prevent overlapping sound— hold Shift as you drag the audio cut point.

Figure 4.10
Offsetting an
audio transition

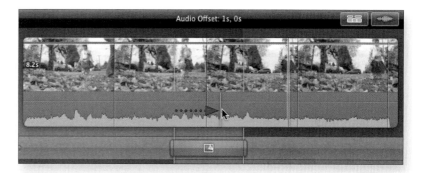

Editing extras in the Precision Editor

 Other elements around the edit point, such as titles or sound effects, can be edited in the Precision Editor, too. Click the Show or Hide Extras button to reveal them (**Figure 4.11**). You can then change their durations or reposition them within the movie; you need to return to the Project browser to perform other edits, such as adjusting clip volume levels or title wording and styles.

Figure 4.11
Editing extras

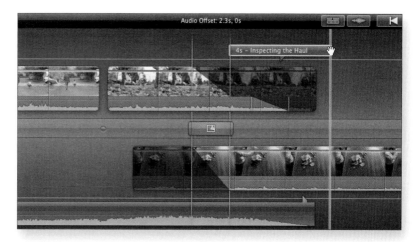

Jump to other edit points without leaving the Precision Editor by clicking the space between clips in the Project browser; by clicking the circle icons in the Precision Editor; or by clicking the Show Previous Edit and Show Next Edit buttons.

Detach audio from a video clip

Nothing says you need to keep audio and video in sync throughout your movie. You may find a bit of dialogue or background noise that you'd like to use over different visuals. In that case, you want to extract the audio clip from its video clip, so you can work with the audio independently. iMovie provides two methods for doing this: detaching audio from a clip in the Project browser, or adding just the audio portion of a clip from the Event browser.

Let's look at a couple of real-world examples. If you encounter unexpected audio in a scene—something drops, a person sneezes—or you just want to maintain an even level of background noise, you can borrow the audio from a different clip and hide the distraction. (Remember in Chapter 1 when I recommended that you record ambient noise when shooting? Here's where it comes in handy.) Or, perhaps you have a great line of dialogue, but the clip's visuals aren't as compelling as another clip's. Here are two methods of using just the audio from other video clips.

Detaching audio from a video clip in the Project browser

1. Locate the clip that has the audio you want to use.

2. Select the clip and choose Clip > Detach Audio, or choose Detach Audio from the contextual menu. A new audio clip appears below the video, and the video track is muted (**Figure 4.12**).

3. Drag the detached audio to the section in your movie where you want it to appear.

   Don't forget to mute or lower the volume on the video clip over which you're adding the new audio.

Figure 4.12
The original clip includes distracting sounds of dishes clattering in this café. The audio from the third clip contains a steady level of background noise.

After detaching the audio to its own clip, I reposition it under the first, noisy, clip. Then, to hide the distractions, I mute the first video clip.

Distracting sounds   *Detached audio clip*

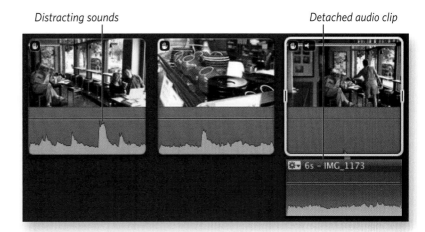

Clip muted

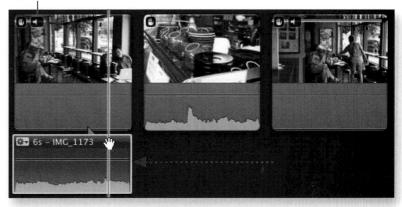

Adding just the audio from a video clip

1. In the Event browser, locate the section of the clip that has the audio you want to use.

2. Drag the selection to the Project browser, dropping it onto the top of a clip where you want the audio to begin.

3. From the pop-up menu that appears, choose Audio Only. The clip appears as an audio clip below the video (**Figure 4.13**).

Figure 4.13
Audio from a video clip added to the project

Create a Photo Slideshow Project

Difficulty level: Easy

Much of this book is focused on bending video to your will, but don't forget that iMovie can also import and work with digital still photos. They're given the "Ken Burns Effect," named after the famed documentary filmmaker who popularized the technique of moving the camera over a still photo to give it a sense of motion. iMovie offers controls for customizing the effect, or ignoring it altogether. You can intersperse photos with video footage or, as I describe here, make a slideshow movie that's composed entirely of photos.

Import photos

If you use iPhoto or Aperture to manage your photo library, or want to grab snapshots from Photo Booth, iMovie can access the photos directly. You can also import photos from the Desktop or other locations on your hard disk.

Importing photos from iPhoto, Aperture, or Photo Booth

1. Click the Photo browser button in the toolbar to view your photo libraries.

2. At the top of the Photo browser, select a photo source. Clicking the disclosure triangle to the left of the application name reveals your events, photos, faces, places, albums, and smart albums in the program (**Figure 4.14**).

Figure 4.14
The Photo browser

3. In the lower portion of the browser, click a photo to preview it in the Viewer.

4. Drag the photo to the Project browser to add it to your movie. A green checkmark appears on the photo thumbnail in the Photo browser to indicate it's in your project.

 To view more thumbnails in the Photo browser, drag the separator between the libraries and the photos. Drag it high enough and the source list becomes a space-saving pop-up menu.

Importing photos from the hard disk

1. Locate the photo you wish to use in the Finder.

2. Drag the photo directly to iMovie's Project browser, dropping it where you want it to appear in the movie (**Figure 4.15**).

Figure 4.15
Importing a photo from the Finder

Adding a source folder to the Photo browser

You can take advantage of the Photo browser even if you don't use iPhoto or Aperture. Drag any folder from the Finder to the top pane of the Photo browser; it appears within a new folder called Folders, and it reveals its images when clicked.

Adjust Ken Burns Effect settings

iMovie automatically applies the Ken Burns Effect to incoming photos. Also known as pan and zoom, the effect makes it appear as if the camera is moving over the surface of the photo, with a gradual zoom in or zoom out. It's a technique that works especially well if you want to focus on something specific, like a person's face, and then back out to reveal their surroundings. You can, of course, change how the effect appears by setting the start and end positions. If you'd rather remove the Ken Burns Effect, jump ahead to "Fit or crop a photo."

Adjusting the Ken Burns Effect

1. Select the photo you wish to edit in the Project browser, and open the photo editing interface in the Viewer by clicking the Crop button on the toolbar; double-clicking the Crop icon in the corner of the photo clip's thumbnail; or pressing the C key (**Figure 4.16**).

Crop icon   *Direction of motion*

Figure 4.16
The Ken Burns Effect editing interface

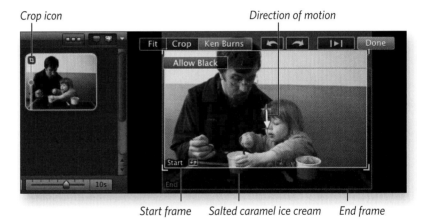

Start frame   Salted caramel ice cream   End frame

2. Drag the corner handles of the green Start rectangle to specify the appearance of the first frame of the effect; the area inside the rectangle will resize to fill the frame when played. Also, drag within the rectangle to reposition it (**Figure 4.17**).

3. Drag the corner handles of the red End rectangle to set the last frame. Click the Play button to preview how it will appear.

4. Want to swap the Start and End positions? Click the Reverse button.

5. Click Done to apply the changes.

Figure 4.17
Setting the Start
and End frames,
and the result

Play button

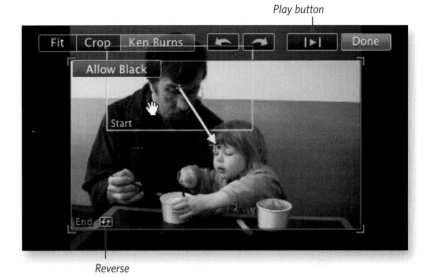

Reverse

Start   End

 Regardless of the original dimensions of the photo, iMovie crops the image to fill the video frame. As you can see in Figure 4.17, that ends up cutting off a fair bit of the image at the top and bottom. If you want to keep the full image in view, albeit with black bars at the sides, click the Allow Black button.

 Now this is clever: When you add multiple photos at once, iMovie reverses the Ken Burns Effect settings for alternate stills. So, if the first photo zooms in, the second photo zooms out, and so on, to make a smooth viewing experience.

Fit or crop a photo

The Ken Burns Effect is snazzy, but too much panning and zooming can give your viewers a headache. If you want to display a photo without movement, set it to be either cropped to the frame or made to fit with black bars visible. The photo controls can also rotate photos, such as portrait-oriented pictures that were not automatically rotated when you imported them from the camera.

Fitting or cropping a photo

1. After adding a picture to your project, view the photo controls (I prefer to double-click the Crop icon or select the clip and press C).

2. Click the Fit button to get as much of the image into frame as possible (**Figure 4.18**).

   Or, click the Crop button and then drag the frame's corners to define the visible area. Cropping is also great when you want to focus on one area of an image and exclude another, just as you would crop a photo in iPhoto.

3. Click Done to apply the changes.

Figure 4.18
Fit and Crop

Fit   *Crop*

 If you set a Crop area and then decide to apply the Ken Burns Effect, the area you defined becomes the Start frame.

Rotating photos

1. Select a photo in your project and bring up the photo controls.

 2. Click the Rotate Counterclockwise or Rotate Clockwise button to turn the photo in 90-degree increments.

3. Click Done.

Change a photo's duration

Incoming photos are given a 4-second duration by default, but you can make them as long as you want. Photos with the Ken Burns Effect applied automatically adjust the timing of the effect based on the clip's duration.

Changing a photo's duration

1. Double-click the photo you want to edit (or press the I key) to bring up the Clip inspector.

2. Enter a new time in the Duration field (**Figure 4.19**).

   If you want all photos in your slideshow to match the same duration, click the "Applies to all stills" checkbox.

3. Click Done.

Figure 4.19
Setting a clip duration

> **tip** In iMovie's Project Properties dialog, you can specify the default behavior of imported photos. For example, every new picture can be set to Crop instead of to the Ken Burns Effect, and can be set at a different duration. Choose File > Project Properties, or press Command-J. Be sure the "Applies when added to project" option is enabled; otherwise the settings apply to all photos already within the project (Figure 4.20).

Figure 4.20
Photo-specific
project settings

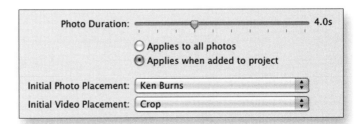

Edit the rest of the slideshow

Now that you know the basics of adding and manipulating still images, continue to edit the rest of the slideshow movie using the editing techniques discussed so far in the book. Rearrange clips to your liking; add transitions, titles, and music; and apply color correction and video effects to photo clips just as you would to video clips (see "Correct Color Project," later in this chapter). (However, although iMovie's color controls are surprisingly powerful, I recommend performing your primary image editing in iPhoto or other software before bringing pictures into iMovie.)

tip   **By far my favorite aspect of iMovie's photo-editing features is this: The settings apply to video as well as to still images. Select a video clip in the Project browser, click the Crop button in the toolbar or press the C key, and you can apply a Ken Burns Effect to video, or crop the clip to remove distractions from the edge of the frame. (Cropping generates better results on HD footage, since the video must be enlarged to fit the frame after you've cropped it, reducing the resolution.)**

Create a Cutaway Project

Difficulty level: Easy

A common video editing technique is to cut between scenes while a consistent section of audio plays. For example, someone is being interviewed, and while you listen to them describe a place they visited, the image switches to video of that place. That clip is called a *cutaway*, and it's easy to create in iMovie. Cutaways are also frequently used as a clever way to hide visual flubs: If you're watching an interview and the camera cuts to the interviewer asking a question, chances are the subject being interviewed had to scratch his or her nose or take a drink of water just then.

Add the cutaway clip

If you've used a video editor such as Final Cut Express, you may miss the capability to overlay clips on multiple video tracks. iMovie offers just one video track—or does it? Although it's not immediately obvious, iMovie does support a second video track for things like cutaways and picture-in-picture effects. That makes implementing a scene like this vastly easier than chopping clips and inserting other clips to accomplish the same task.

Adding a cutaway

1. In the Event browser, select a section of clip you want to use as the cutaway.

2. Drag the selection to the spot in your movie where the cutaway begins, dropping it directly onto the clip.

3. From the pop-up menu that appears, choose Cutaway (**Figure 4.21**).

Figure 4.21
Adding a cutaway

The cutaway appears above the main video track. A shaded area indicates video is hidden in favor of the cutaway clip (**Figure 4.22**).

Cutaway clip

Figure 4.22
The cutaway
in the project

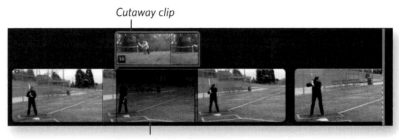

Footage hidden by cutaway

The advantage to this approach is that you can reposition or trim the cutaway clip without having to touch the base video clip at all. And because the cutaway is just a regular video clip, you can perform other edits and effects on it.

Edit the cutaway clip settings

You can also edit a couple of attributes that are specific to cutaway clips: whether it appears suddenly or with a fade-in (and disappears with a fade-out), and the opacity of the clip.

Applying a fade transition to a cutaway

1. Double-click a cutaway clip, or select it and press the I key, to bring up the Clip inspector.

2. Change the Cutaway Fade setting to Manual, and optionally change the duration of the fade (**Figure 4.23**). This setting applies to the start and end of the clip, and your only option is to fade the clip; you can't choose other transition styles.

Figure 4.23
Cutaway-specific settings

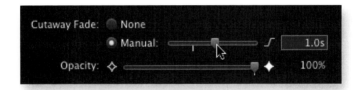

Changing the clip's opacity

In the Clip inspector, drag the Opacity slider to adjust how transparent the clip appears (perfect for scenes of ghostly apparitions).

Create a Picture in Picture or Side by Side Scene Project

Difficulty level: Easy

Similar to a cutaway, the Picture in Picture feature provides the opportunity to display a second clip without disrupting the main video, only in this case the clip appears in a box in the corner of the screen. Another option is the Side by Side effect, which splits the screen to display two clips at once.

Add the Picture in Picture or Side by Side clip

Creating a Picture in Picture or Side by Side clip works the same way as creating a cutaway, with the clip appearing above the main video track. In the case of the Picture in Picture effect, other controls are also available.

Adding a Picture in Picture or Side by Side clip

1. Select a range of video from the Event browser and drag it onto a clip in your project.

2. Choose Picture in Picture or Side by Side from the pop-up menu.

3. If you added a Picture in Picture clip, go to the Viewer and drag the clip to change its location within the frame. You can also resize the box by dragging the corner handles (**Figure 4.24**).

Figure 4.24
Resizing a Picture in Picture clip

Edit the clip settings

Double-click the Picture in Picture or Side by Side clip to bring up the Clip inspector, where you'll find settings specific to each effect, such as the option to apply a border style to the Picture in Picture clip.

Setting Picture in Picture options

- **PIP Effect:** This option controls how the picture box appears. From the pop-up menu, choose Dissolve for a fade-in effect, or Zoom to enlarge the box from a corner. Then, set a duration for the effect using the slider (**Figure 4.25**).

The PIP Effect pop-up menu also includes a curious gem: Swap. When that's enabled, the Picture in Picture clip occupies the entire frame while the base clip appears in the box.

Figure 4.25
Settings for Picture in Picture

- **Border Width:** Click a button to specify no border (the default) or a thin or thick border around the box.

- **Border Color:** "Color" is a bit of a stretch here, but if the Border Width is set to thin or thick, use this option to set the border as black, gray, or white.

- **Drop Shadow:** Click the Visible checkbox to make the box cast a subtle shadow.

Setting Side by Side options

- **Side by Side:** Choose on which side of the screen the Side by Side clip should appear, left or right (**Figure 4.26**).

- **Slide:** Click the Manual button and adjust the duration slider to make the clip slide into frame from the side specified in the pop-up menu.

Figure 4.26
Side by Side settings

Stabilize Shaky Footage Project

Difficulty level: Easy

Not too long ago, if your footage exhibited camera shake—that slight bouncing or jittery motion introduced by shooting with a lightweight camera—either you compensated by locking the camera to a tripod, or you accepted the shaky video and passed it off as "edgy." Now, iMovie can analyze and stabilize that footage.

Analyze for image stabilization

To smooth shaky video, iMovie analyzes each frame to identify similar objects. Then, it figures out how much zoom and rotation to apply to each frame to make the objects line up, effectively removing the shake.

Given that most clips contain 24 or 30 frames per second, analyzing for stabilization can take quite a while—four to eight times the duration of the original footage, or potentially several hours if you analyze a lot of video in one batch. Fortunately, you have several opportunities to perform the analysis, allowing you to analyze a large batch at once, or smaller sections as you edit.

Analyzing a clip for stabilization

You can analyze video at any of the following points:

- When you add video to iMovie, click the "After import analyze for Stabilization" checkbox in the Import dialog. iMovie scans all the footage being imported, tying up the program until it's finished. This is a good option to use if you want to import a lot of video overnight while you're sleeping.

- Select a clip in the Event browser and choose File > Analyze Video > Stabilization. The entire clip is analyzed, even if you've selected only a portion of it. (You can also choose to analyze for stabilization and people in the same pass.)

- Select a clip in the Project browser and choose File > Analyze Video > Stabilization. iMovie scans just the section in your movie, not the entire clip in the Event browser. However, if you add more video from the same clip in your project, iMovie analyzes it again.

- Double-click a clip to bring up the Clip inspector. If the clip is in the Event browser, click the Analyze Entire Clip button (**Figure 4.27**). If you've selected a clip in the Project browser, click the "Stabilization: Smooth clip motion" checkbox.

Figure 4.27
Stabilization button in the inspector

 If you have the time, I recommend analyzing clips in a large batch, such as during import. That enables you to apply stabilization during editing without having to wait for iMovie to scan footage on the fly.

Apply image stabilization

With your footage analyzed, you can control how much stabilization is applied. iMovie doesn't actually re-render the video; instead, it keeps track of how much zoom and rotation each frame needs to match surrounding frames.

Applying image stabilization

 If the footage was previously analyzed in the Event browser, all you need to do is add the clip to your project; stabilization is automatically applied, indicated by an icon in the corner of the clip. For any clip in the Project browser that isn't yet analyzed, open the Clip inspector (double-click the clip, or select it and press the I key) and enable the "Stabilization: Smooth clip motion" checkbox.

To control the amount of stabilization applied, drag the Maximum Zoom slider in the Clip inspector. iMovie assumes you want the most stable footage, but you may want to ease back on the setting occasionally. If the clip has a lot of motion, iMovie must zoom further in to get frames to match up—sometimes cutting out important sections of the scene, like slicing off the tops of people's heads (**Figure 4.28**).

Figure 4.28
Maximum Zoom
settings compared

tip

Some portions of clips contain too much camera shake for iMovie to compensate. You'll see a squiggly red line to indicate those frames (Figure 4.29). To hide those sections, click the Hide Excessive Shake button.

Figure 4.29
Excessive shake

Hide Excessive Shake button   *Excessive shake indicator*

Compensate for rolling shutter

Many of today's cameras use CMOS sensors, which record each frame in horizontal lines, scanning from top to bottom. When camera shake or sudden movement is introduced during shooting, the objects in the video appear "bendy," like they're made of rubber, due to an effect called *rolling shutter*. Although the best advice is to try to capture steady video in the first place, iMovie can help take the elasticity out of the clips (although the effectiveness varies widely, depending on the source footage).

Compensating for rolling shutter

1. Make sure the clip you're editing has been analyzed for stabilization, and then open the Clip inspector.

2. Under Rolling Shutter, click the "Reduce motion distortion" checkbox (**Figure 4.30**).

3. Choose a setting from the Amount pop-up menu; iMovie defaults to Medium, but try the other amounts to see if they improve the clip.

Figure 4.30
Rolling Shutter settings

Correct Color Project

Difficulty level: Intermediate

As you know, the way to get the best picture when you shoot is to start with great original footage. However, that's not always possible; maybe the white balance was set wrong, or lighting shifted while filming. Or, perhaps you just want to increase the saturation of a clip to make it pop. iMovie's color correction tools are surprisingly effective, and they can help you tweak your image in subtle or strong ways.

The program also offers several video effects for when you want to dramatically change the appearance of your clips, from making them grayscale to applying an X-ray look.

Correct a clip's color

If you've used the color correction tools in iPhoto, you'll be familiar with the controls in iMovie.

Correcting color

1. Select a clip to edit; corrections apply to entire clips, so if you want to affect just a portion of a clip, you need to first split the section into its own clip.

2. Open the Video inspector by double-clicking the clip and clicking the Video button in the inspector, or by just pressing the V key.

3. I recommend letting iMovie take the first stab at fixing color: Click the Auto button. If the clip looks good to you, click the Done button to close the inspector. Or, continue to the next step.

4. Using the controls in the inspector, make any of the following adjustments (**Figure 4.31**):

Figure 4.31
Controls in the Video inspector

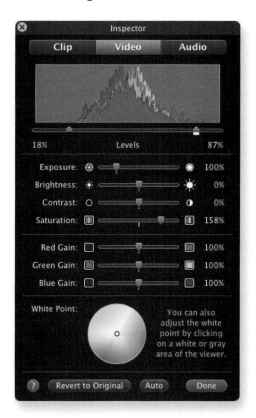

- **Levels.** The histogram at the top of the window represents the levels of red, blue, and green in the current frame. The sliders below the graph represent the darkest and lightest values (pure black or white).

  Drag the left slider toward the middle to darken the image; drag the right slider similarly to lighten the image. Doing so treats the furthermost colors on the outside edges as darkest or lightest.

- **Exposure.** This slider brightens or darkens the video's highlights.

- **Brightness.** This slider controls the overall lightness of the clip.

- **Contrast.** Accentuate the differences between light and dark.

- **Saturation.** Drag this slider to change the color intensity.

- **Gain sliders.** Adjust these slider values to compensate for color casts (to reduce a green tint, for example). The Gain sliders appear only when Show Advanced Tools is enabled in iMovie's preferences.

- **White Point.** This control tells iMovie which color value equals white; the rest of the colors are based on that value. Move the point within the color wheel to adjust the white point, which can also affect the clip's color cast. Or, click within the Viewer to specify which color should be treated as white (it also bases its settings on gray values).

- **Revert to Original.** If you don't like the adjustments you made, click here to go back to the original settings.

For an example of the color adjustment controls in action, I used the settings in Figure 4.31 to bring out detail and color in an otherwise washed-out clip (**Figure 4.32**).

Figure 4.32
Color correction applied

Original   *Corrected*

Color correction can be applied to clips in both the Project browser and the Event browser. So, you can adjust color before adding anything to your movie if you choose.

Apply video effects

If you're looking for an easier way to change the appearance of a clip, choose from iMovie's collection of 19 premade video effects.

Applying video effects

1. Select the clip you want to adjust.

2. Double-click the clip to bring up the Clip inspector.

3. Click the Video Effect button, which exposes a grid of the available effects.

4. Move your mouse over each effect to preview its appearance in the Viewer before making your choice (**Figure 4.33**).

5. Click the effect you want to use to apply it.

Figure 4.33
Previewing a
video effect

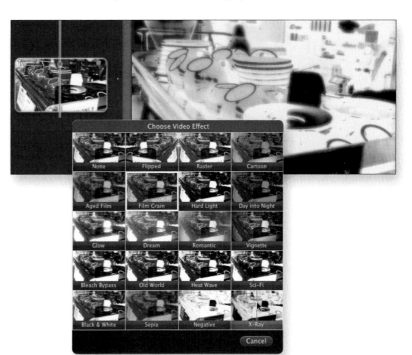

With the effects picker visible, press the spacebar to play the selected clip in a loop. As you move your mouse pointer over the effects, the preview continues to play, using the option currently under the pointer to give you a better idea of how the effect works on the entire clip, not just one frame.

 Unfortunately, you can apply only one video effect at a time, with one exception. If you want to make a clip black and white, and then apply an effect on top of that, do this: In the Video inspector, first drag the Saturation slider down to zero. Then, go to the Clip inspector and choose a video effect.

To remove an effect, bring up the Choose Video Effect window again and click the None option.

Change How a Clip Sounds Project

Difficulty level: Intermediate

Just as you can apply video effects to a clip, you can change how audio sounds by using several preset effects. Or, if you're looking for subtler options, you can adjust the volume of background clips ("ducking"), change the audio balance using an equalizer, and filter background noise.

Apply audio effects

Want to make a scene sound like it's in a larger room than the one in which you shot it? Make a person sound like they are talking on the telephone or were transported from another planet? iMovie's audio effects range from fanciful to practical.

Applying audio effects

1. Click the clip you want to edit.

2. Open the Clip inspector, and then click the Audio Effects button to bring up the Choose Audio Effect dialog (**Figure 4.34**). iMovie automatically starts playing a preview of the clip.

Figure 4.34
Make Planet Claire
sound like a real
cosmic thing using
audio effects.

3. Move your mouse pointer over an effect name to hear how it changes the audio.

4. Click the effect you want to use.

"Duck" a clip

Often, if someone is talking in a scene, you don't want the volume of background music to drown out the dialogue. Using iMovie's ducking feature, the background audio can automatically be lowered so it doesn't compete. When the foreground clip ends, the background audio comes back up, without you having to make the adjustments manually.

Ducking a clip

1. Select the clip that you want to remain at regular volume.

2. Bring up the Audio inspector by double-clicking the clip and clicking the Audio button, or by pressing the A key.

3. Click the Ducking checkbox (**Figure 4.35**).

Figure 4.35
The Ducking checkbox
and slider

4. Adjust the slider to specify the volume level of other tracks that appear with the selected clip (**Figure 4.36**).

Figure 4.36
The volume of the background song is reduced after ducking is enabled for the video clip.

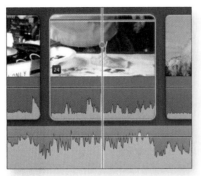 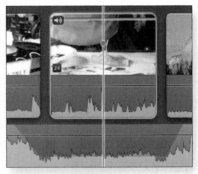

Normal   *With ducking applied*

Change equalizer settings

It's not the same as the giant mixing boards you'll find in a sound studio, but iMovie's equalizer can help you shape your clips' audio. Presets like Voice Enhance, Music Enhance, and Hum Reduction are tailored to the sound recorded by video cameras.

Changing equalizer settings

1. Select a clip you want to edit.

2. Open the Audio inspector by double-clicking the clip and then clicking the Audio button in the inspector, or by pressing the A key.

3. From the Equalizer pop-up menu, choose a preset (**Figure 4.37**). Or, mark the Equalizer checkbox and adjust the sliders manually.

Figure 4.37
Equalizer presets

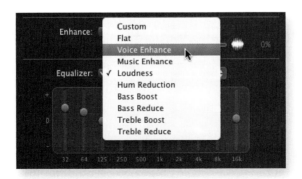

tip Another common audio problem you're likely to run into is varying volume levels among all clips in a movie. One thing to try is normalizing the clips: Select one, bring up the Audio inspector, and click the Normalize Clip Volume button.

Reduce background noise

If your video contains a persistent hiss or hum, or if there's just enough background white noise in an environment to be distracting, you can filter the noise in iMovie. I've found this feature to be hit or miss, so it really depends on the audio in the clip—it's better at minimizing subtle white noise than something more specific like wind noise. Still, it's worth a try, and it's easy to enable.

Reducing background noise

1. Select a clip you want to edit.

2. Open the Audio inspector by double-clicking the clip and then clicking the Audio button in the inspector, or by pressing the A key.

3. In the Enhance section, enable the "Reduce background noise by" checkbox and drag the slider to specify a percentage of the effect to apply (**Figure 4.38**).

Figure 4.38
Reducing background noise

5

Creative iMovie Projects

I've covered a lot of ground so far, and hopefully by now you have not only a good foundation for how to edit in iMovie, but also the confidence to try new things and explore features that aren't obvious. In this chapter, I get more creative, using a variety of techniques to create a travel highlights movie, demonstrate how to incorporate green-screen special effects, create a music video, make a sports highlight video using iMovie's clever Sports Team Editor, and build a custom soundtrack for a movie using the looping capabilities of GarageBand.

Make a Music Video Project

Difficulty: Intermediate

So far in this book, when working with music, you've added music to a previously edited movie. Perhaps if you're the creative type, you've already played with editing your movie a bit to sync more closely with the music, but even in that case, the movie came first. In some instances, though, you may want to start with the music. Music videos are a great example, where the visuals serve the beat.

 Music videos are only one example of where this technique might be useful. Slideshows, montage and action sequences, and movie trailers are other examples of when this technique could be useful. In fact, iMovie's movie trailers feature, at heart, uses the techniques described here, just in a more guided interface.

Use beat markers

To start with the music and work from there, use iMovie's beat markers. This feature lets you build a project full of edit points and then populate the movie with video and photo clips, which are all automatically cut to the markers.

Making a music video using beat markers

1. Choose File > New Project to create a new project.

2. Enable Snap to Beats under the View menu, if it's not already active.

 3. Click the Music and Sound Effects Browser button, or press Command-1, to access your music library.

4. Choose a song from your iTunes playlist and drag it to the Project browser (**Figure 5.1**).

5. Click the song's Action menu and choose Clip Trimmer to open it.

Figure 5.1
Adding a song to an
empty project

6. Add beat markers using one of the following techniques:

    • Using the audio waveform as a guide, create a new beat marker
    by dragging a marker from the Beat Marker icon to the clip
    (**Figure 5.2**).

    • Play the song by pressing the spacebar or the backslash (\) key,
    and then press the M key whenever you want to add a beat
    marker. Don't worry about being exact—you can move the
    markers later.

Figure 5.2
Drag from the Beat
Marker icon to add a
new beat marker.

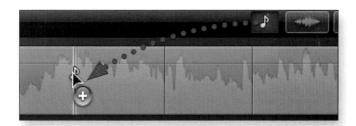

tip **Think like an editor while you add markers. If you add too many
markers you'll end up with a bunch of really quick edits (although
that may be the effect you want).**

7. Play through your song and make sure all the beat markers are
where you want them. If you need to adjust one, click and drag it.
To delete a marker, drag it out of the Clip Trimmer; or, bring up the
contextual menu and choose Remove Beat Marker.

note If you don't see Remove Beat Marker in the contextual menu, you're not hovering close enough to the marker. Click outside of the menu to close it and try again. You can also Control-click an empty part of the song and add a beat marker by selecting Add Beat Marker.

8. Once all your markers are in place, click Done to close the Clip Trimmer.

9. Add video clips to the project, either individually or in groups. iMovie automatically trims them to fit between your beat markers (**Figure 5.3**).

Figure 5.3
Clips added are trimmed at the beat markers.

tip I often find it's easiest to roughly define clip selections, drag them into the project, and then open them in the Clip Trimmer to precisely edit the selection. This enables me to work more quickly and to synchronize the clip selections with the music more closely.

tip For most music videos, you want the song to be the only audio playing. To quickly mute the video clips in the project, select them all and choose Clip > Mute Clips or press Command-Shift-M.

Editing beat markers after clips are placed

1. Select the background music track and open it in the Clip Trimmer.

2. With Snap to Beats still enabled in the View menu, do any of the following:

   • Drag a new beat marker to the track. iMovie splits the clip that's bisected by the new marker.

   • Drag a beat marker to a new location. iMovie adjusts the durations of affected clips to accommodate the change.

   • Delete a beat marker. iMovie asks how you'd like to deal with the edit at that spot (**Figure 5.4**).

Figure 5.4
iMovie needs guidance when you delete a beat marker.

Remove Beat Marker

What would you like to do with the edit associated with this beat marker?

Cancel   Extend Left   Extend Right   Leave As-Is

tip

As much as possible, perform a first edit of your music video using the beat markers and the Clip Trimmer. If you delete a clip in the Project browser, iMovie warns that doing so can knock everything out of sync.

Fine-tuning the edits

With the clips you want to use in place, edit them using the techniques described in Chapter 4. For example, use the Replace edits to swap one clip for another; or, to use a different portion of the same clip, open the clip in the Clip Trimmer and drag using the bottom of the selection border to make the other portion visible while still maintaining the clip's duration. The Precision Editor is especially helpful, because you can see how clip edges interact at the edit point.

Record a Voiceover Project

Difficulty: Easy

Narrators are often maligned in dramatic films—it's commonly an indi-cation that the screenwriter or director got sloppy and needed to employ a narrator to help explain the story. But in documentary films they can be essential. Imagine *March of the Penguins* without Morgan Freeman's mellifluous narration.

Record audio using the Voiceover tool

Whether you're adding detail to vacation highlights or explaining some-thing technical, you can record audio directly into the iMovie timeline.

 Modern Macs include built-in microphones, but you'll get *much* **better results if you use an external mic. The built-in ones are designed for chat-ting via audio or video, not for making audio recordings of any quality. The easiest way to attach an external microphone is to use a USB mic. Many models are available, from expensive options by SE Electronics, Rode, and MXL, to more affordable ones by Logitech and Blue.**

Recording audio

1. Connect a microphone to your Mac, if necessary.

 2. Click the Voiceover button in the toolbar, or press the O key, to open the Voiceover window (**Figure 5.5**).

Figure 5.5
Audio levels in the Voiceover window

3. Choose an input source from the Record From pop-up window.

4. Speak into the microphone and adjust the Input Volume slider so the meters show a strong signal but remain green.

5. Drag the Noise Reduction slider to the right to filter out ambient noise.

6. The Voice Enhancement checkbox enables an algorithm to electronically smooth spoken word recordings; uncheck the box if you prefer your voice to be unaltered (definitely experiment to see which you prefer).

7. Enable the "Play project audio while recording" checkbox if you're listening through headphones and need to hear audio cues from your movie while you record.

8. To begin recording, click the point on the filmstrip where you want the audio to start. iMovie gives you a 3-second countdown before it starts to record.

9. Speak into the microphone. The filmstrip turns red to indicate where you've recorded (**Figure 5.6**).

Figure 5.6
Recording a voiceover

10. Click anywhere within the Project browser or press the spacebar to stop recording. A new purple audio clip appears (**Figure 5.7**).

Figure 5.7
The voiceover appears as a purple audio clip.

tip Make sure you click the clip or press the spacebar to stop recording; if you close the Voiceover window (or press the O key), your recording isn't saved.

11. The Voiceover tool remains active; to record another clip, click another spot in the filmstrip.

    You can record multiple takes and then delete the ones you don't like (**Figure 5.8**). Be aware that when you play your project back you'll hear all your takes at once unless you mute some of them.

12. When you're finished recording, click the close button on the Voiceover window to close it, or press the Esc key.

Figure 5.8
Feel free to record multiple takes.

tip Voiceover recordings are regular audio clips, which means you can edit them like any other clip. If the beginning of one recording sounds great but includes a flub later, you can trim away the error and record just the section you need (Figure 5.9).

Figure 5.9
Mix and match voice-over recordings to get the best result.

Create a Travel Highlights Movie Project

Difficulty: Easy

The modern version of iMovie was designed for making travel videos. I'm being literal: An Apple engineer went on a diving vacation and wanted a better, faster way to cut together the footage he shot. Although iMovie is used for making everything from family videos to school projects, my guess is that a majority of movies out there relate people's epic vacation adventures. This project uses a theme to provide structure, and includes an animated map to show where you've been.

Create a travel-themed project

Although applying a theme for the project is entirely optional, it provides a framework for your movie and automatically adds many titles and transitions.

Creating a project and applying a theme

1. Choose File > New Project (or press Command-N) to create the new project.

2. Click a theme to choose it; in this case, I'm using the Bulletin Board theme as an example (**Figure 5.10**).

Figure 5.10
Choosing a project theme

3. Enable the "Automatically add transitions and titles" checkbox below the theme preview. This, too, is optional, but part of the point with the project is to let iMovie do some of the heavy lifting.

4. Click the Create button to create the project.

5. Drag clips from the Event browser to the Project browser to build your movie. As you do, notice that themed titles and transitions automatically appear (**Figure 5.11**). In fact, iMovie keeps them organized: If you add a clip to the beginning of the movie, the theme title shifts to the first clip.

Figure 5.11
Theme elements are added automatically.

Theme title   *Theme transition*

 tip   **Each theme includes a handful of different title and transition types. Open the Titles or Transitions browser to view theme-specific options above the standard complement of options.**

Add a map

In one of my early travel videos, I painstakingly attempted to replicate the Indiana Jones-style map where a line progresses from location to location on a map to indicate our travel route. Now, iMovie makes it extremely easy.

Adding a map

1. Click the Maps, Backgrounds, and Animatics button to view the available maps.

2. Drag one of the maps from the browser to a spot in your project. (Only the top two rows of maps are animated.)

3. In the inspector that appears, iMovie fills in your current location (if it knows it) as the Start Location (**Figure 5.12**).

Figure 5.12
Map-specific options in the inspector

4. Click the Choose End Location button to specify a destination.

5. Enter the name of a city, airport, or major landmark and choose from the list of results that appears. You can also customize the name in the "Name to display on map" field.

6. Click Done to finish editing the map.

 Easily change the map style by dragging a different map onto the map in the Project browser.

 When you add a map in the Bulletin Board theme, the maps that appear in the background of the theme transitions change to match the style of the one you added.

Edit the Content of Theme Transitions

Some themes feature the capability to customize the contents of the transitions. Bulletin Board, for example, pulls images from elsewhere in your project to use as the photos that are pinned to the board. To choose which items are included, do the following:

1. Select a transition in the Project browser. A full view of the transition image (which normally appears zoomed) includes numbered image areas.

2. In the Project browser, drag one of the numbered flags to an area of your movie to use that frame in the transition image (**Figure 5.13**).

3. Click Done to apply the changes.

Figure 5.13
Editing transition elements

Image marker   *Image in transition*

Create a Sports Highlights Movie Project

Difficulty: Intermediate

Almost as soon as I started writing about iMovie years ago, I started to receive questions from parents and coaches who were using iMovie to create weekly recaps of sporting events for their teams to watch and learn from. iMovie '11 includes a new feature, the Sports Team Editor, an internal team database you can access for such sports highlight movies.

Build the sports team database

iMovie's Sports Team Editor is designed to keep track of your team and be available for upcoming videos.

Entering team information into the Sports Team Editor

1. Choose Window > Sports Team Editor to open the editor.

2. Click the Create a New Team button, and enter a season and team name and choose the sport (**Figure 5.14**).

3. If you want to include a team logo, click the + button in the Team Logo field and locate an image file on disk.

Figure 5.14
Setting up your very own sports franchise

Create a new team

4. In the Players section, click the Create a New Player button.

5. Enter the player's name, position, and other information, and add a player photo (**Figure 5.15**).

6. Click Done to exit the Sports Team Editor.

Figure 5.15
Adding players
to the team

Create a new player

The default player information is pretty generic, but you can customize the columns. Click the expansion triangle next to Sports at the bottom of the window, and double-click a label for your sport to change it.

If you already track your team information in a spreadsheet or other database, export the data to a tab-delimited text file. You can then import that into the Sports Team Editor and save some time.

Add Sports theme elements

The Sports Team Editor, unsurprisingly, ties into iMovie's Sports theme, with some transitions that take advantage of the player information.

Adding Sports theme elements

Create a new project using the Sports theme. If you've already created a project, you can switch to the Sports theme by choosing File > Project Theme (or pressing Command-Shift-J).

If the option to automatically add transitions and titles is enabled, iMovie creates those items on its own. However, the coolest ones are titles that need to be added manually. Open the Titles browser and check out the following:

- **Score.** Add this title to drop a game score summary from the top of the screen. In the pop-ups that appear in the Viewer, specify each team and then enter a number in the score fields provided.

- **Team vs Team.** Good for placing near the front of the video, this title lets you choose which teams are playing and displays their logos.

- **Player Stats.** Add this title to overlay a player's information. Choose the player in the pop-up menu that appears (**Figure 5.16**).

Figure 5.16
Adding a Player Stats
title to a clip

 If you change any information in the Sports Team Editor, an alert appears at the bottom of the window informing you that the project contains outdated team information and needs to be updated. Click the Update Project button.

Make a Green-Screen Effect Project

Difficulty: Intermediate

I'll admit it, one reason I go to see summer Hollywood movies is the special effects. Compared to effects just 20 years ago, what artists can do with pixels now is amazing. Now, I won't pretend that you can get that level of quality in iMovie, but you can take footage shot against a green screen or a blue screen and project something else in its place. Imagine shooting a video podcast, or creating a school report where your child stands in front of a diagram and points to key sections of it. Or really, just imagine yourself in a galaxy far, far away...

 Why green or blue? iMovie looks for a broad range of color, so if you happen to be wearing something that's green, you'd want to use a blue screen; use a green screen if something in the video is blue.

Shoot against a green or blue screen

The first thing you need is some green or blue material to drape behind your subject. That can be an inexpensive piece of cloth from a fabric store or even a wall or board painted a solid color. Any area that's green or blue will be rendered invisible when you add it to your iMovie project (**Figure 5.17**).

Figure 5.17
Green screen for all your dramatic readings

When setting up the scene, try not to project harsh shadows on the background. Also try to avoid items with reflective surfaces that might pick up some of the green color.

When shooting the green-screen footage, move out of the frame at the end of a scene so the camera records a few frames of just the area with the green screen. iMovie can use that to better identify areas that should be masked.

Add a green-screen clip to your movie

A green-screen clip works similar to a cutaway (described in Chapter 4) in that it overlays other footage in your project. When you add it as a green-screen or blue-screen clip, those colors are knocked out.

Adding a green-screen clip to your movie

1. Add the clip that will be visible in the background. That can be regular footage, a photo, or even one of the backgrounds found in the Maps, Backgrounds, and Animatics browser.

2. Drag a clip shot against the screen from the Event browser onto one of the background clips.

3. From the pop-up menu that appears, choose Green Screen or Blue Screen (depending on the screen color you shot) (**Figure 5.18**).

Figure 5.18
Adding the clip as Green Screen

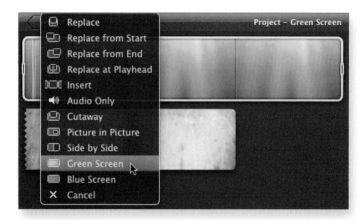

iMovie automatically removes the green or blue areas, which you can see in the Viewer (**Figure 5.19**).

Figure 5.19
Just another weeknight under the sea.

Improve the green-screen effect

iMovie doesn't have the advanced features found in professional compositing software, but there are a few things you can do to try to improve the appearance of the green-screen effect.

Cropping areas

1. If there are areas in the clip that aren't important, such as around the edges, first select the green-screen clip in the Project browser.

2. In the Viewer, click the Cropped button to display corner handles.

3. Drag the handles to mask out areas that you're sure will not contain any of the clip's content (**Figure 5.20**).

Non-green area   *Cropping handle*

Figure 5.20
I unintentionally included an area outside the green screen when shooting, which isn't hidden (left). Cropping that edge removes the gaffe (right).

 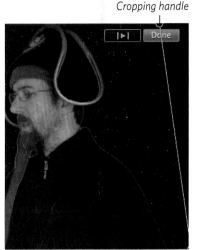

Using the Subtract Last Frame feature

Earlier I suggested that you step out of the frame when recording and capture the green screen by itself. That's to take advantage of the Subtract Last Frame feature, where iMovie performs some extra color cleanup using that frame as a guide.

1. Add the green-screen clip to your project.

2. Double-click the clip to bring up the Clip inspector.

3. Go to the Background settings and enable the Subtract Last Frame option, and then click Done. iMovie uses the frame as a reference to remove more color (**Figure 5.21**).

Figure 5.21
By itself, the green-screen clip gave iMovie some trouble around the book (left). With Subtract Last Frame enabled, the noise disappeared.

 One other technique to improve the mask is to adjust the green or blue gain sliders in the Video inspector. Your mileage will definitely vary, but it's worth a try.

Create a Score in GarageBand Project

Difficulty: Intermediate

Software needed: GarageBand '11

You've already used iMovie's built-in audio clips and imported songs into a movie from your iTunes library, but what if you want something original? If you own both iMovie and GarageBand (either purchased separately through the App Store or as part of the iLife '11 package), you have all the tools you need to create your own soundtrack—even if you don't know a lick about making music.

GarageBand ships with thousands of short audio snippets called loops, brief segments of music that can be repeated—looped—to create sections of a song. They're typically played by one instrument or instrumental group, like a guitar, a drum kit, or a horn section. By layering and combining various loops, you can quickly and easily create a unique composition. For this project, you'll need a movie that's roughly two to three minutes in length.

tip I highly recommend two excellent books by my colleague Jeff Tolbert. If you're new to GarageBand, read *Take Control of Making Music with GarageBand '11*. If you already know how to play an instrument, you need (yes, need) *Take Control of Recording with GarageBand '11* (www.takecontrolbooks.com/news/garageband).

Get your movie into GarageBand

As you work to build a soundtrack for your movie, obviously you want to be able to reference the footage. To do that, you can import a version of the movie directly into GarageBand as its own track.

Preparing the movie for export

1. In iMovie's Project Library, select the project you want to work on.

2. Choose Share > Media Browser. The Media Browser is a library of media shared by many other programs, including the iLife and iWork applications.

3. Choose an export size. I recommend picking a low-resolution version, because ultimately you're going to bring the completed score back into iMovie.

   (It is possible to send the movie to GarageBand and export the final version from there, but it involves an extra layer of video compression between your original and the end result.)

4. Click the Publish button. iMovie creates the shared version of the movie for the Media Browser. (GarageBand doesn't recognize iMovie projects that have not been shared to the Media Browser.)

Opening your movie in GarageBand

1. Launch GarageBand.

2. In the New Project dialog, choose Movie.

3. Click the Choose button. The New Project from Template dialog appears, basically a Save As dialog box with a few extra features (**Figure 5.22**, on the next page).

Figure 5.22
Save the file and
set the key.

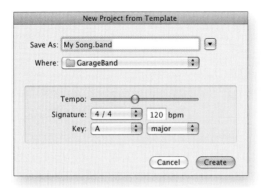

4. Enter a name for your project in the Save As field.

5. Choose a folder in the Where pop-up menu. Your GarageBand folder is a great default location.

6. Change the Key setting to A major.

I'm changing the key to A major here because I know I'm going to use certain loops that sound better in the key of A. This is not something you normally have to do when you create a project. You can always change the key later, too.

7. Click Create. The main GarageBand window opens with a Movie track already in place and the Media Browser open (**Figure 5.23**).

Figure 5.23
GarageBand with a
Movie track

8. In the Movies tab of the Media Browser, select iMovie from the pop-up menu.

9. Locate the movie project you shared to the Media Browser and drag it into the timeline (**Figure 5.24**).

   GarageBand takes a moment to build thumbnails for your movie and then displays it in the timeline. Your movie's audio appears in a separate Movie Sound track.

Figure 5.24
Adding the movie to the Movie track

> **tip**
> If you look carefully, you'll notice a tiny preview of your video in the Movie Track header, to the left of the movie thumbnails. To see a bigger preview, double-click the thumbnail to open it in a larger floating window (Figure 5.25).

Figure 5.25
View a larger preview of your movie.

Start creating your first song

Now that your movie is in place, it's time to start building some music. In order to do that, we need to get all the extraneous panes out of the way and open the Loop browser.

 I'm being more detailed than usual in this project, specifying particular loops to use by way of example. Feel free to follow along, or use the tutorial as a general indicator of how to build your own score.

Opening the Loop browser

 1. Choose Control > Hide Editor or click the Editor button to hide the editor. (The editor allows you to add markers and chapters to your movie track, and enables more precise editing of audio tracks.)

 A "track" in GarageBand refers to a discrete lane of audio data. Each track usually carries a separate musical instrument, and you can independently adjust each track's volume and effects without affecting other tracks in the song.

 2. Choose Control > Show Loop Browser or click the Loop Browser button to show the Loop browser.

The Loop browser, as the name implies, is where GarageBand stores all of its loops. Looking for a drum beat or a guitar riff? This is where you'll find it!

3. For this piece, you're going to start with an acoustic guitar. Click the Guitars button in the top half of the Loop browser. A list of available loops appears in the list below.

Adding your first loops

1. If you needed to download the extra loops, relaunch GarageBand, open the Loop browser, and click the Guitars button to get back to where you left off.

2. In the results list, scroll down to find Picked Steel String 01. Clicking its name plays a preview.

If you don't see **Picked Steel String 01** in the results list, your song may not be in the correct key. Click the icon in the LCD and switch to the Project mode (**Figure 5.26**). Change the key to A major.

Figure 5.26
Switching to the Project mode in order to change key

3. Drag the loop to the timeline, making sure it starts at the beginning of the movie (**Figure 5.27**). GarageBand creates a new track called Acoustic Guitar, and a blue region appears in the timeline.

Figure 5.27
Adding a loop to the project

 Regions are the GarageBand equivalent of clips. They each hold a discrete chunk of music or audio. Like iMovie clips, two regions can butt up against one another, but they can't overlap.

4. Click the icon in the LCD and switch to Measures mode. A measure is a segment of musical time measured in beats. This piece, like many pieces of Western music, has four beats per measure. Working in measures makes it much easier to align regions to create a song.

Download the Extra GarageBand Content

When you first install GarageBand, the program doesn't automatically include all of its available loops. If many of your loop choices are grayed out and have little arrows next to them, you haven't yet downloaded the additional 1.2 GB of loops and instruments. Follow these instructions to install GarageBand's complete collection of loops and instruments:

1. In the Loop browser results list, look for a loop that's dimmed and has an arrow next to its name—for example, Acoustic Picking 01—and click the arrow.

2. In the dialog box that appears, choose to download the extra content now and click OK. Software Update opens and checks for other available updates.

3. When Software Update appears, choose the items you want to download. If there are multiple items and you're pressed for time, you can choose to install only GarageBand Instruments and Apple Loops.

4. Click the Install button. Once the download is complete, you'll need to quit and restart Garage-Band to complete the installation.

5. Hover the cursor over the upper-right corner of the Picked Steel String 01 region. Notice how the cursor changes into a circular arrow, called the loop pointer.

6. With the loop pointer still over the upper-right corner of the region, click and drag to the right. The region duplicates itself—it loops—to fill the space under the cursor.

7. Drag right to loop the region four times. The end of the region should line up with the 5 on the beat ruler, above the movie thumbnails (**Figure 5.28**).

 Make sure Control > Snap to Grid is checked. This makes moving, looping, and aligning regions much easier.

8. Hit the Return key to make sure the playhead is at the beginning of the movie.

9. Press the spacebar or click the Play button to hear the beginning of your piece.

   The song is not very exciting yet, but it's a start. In the next section, you're going to add more loops and start building an actual song.

Figure 5.28
Loop de loop

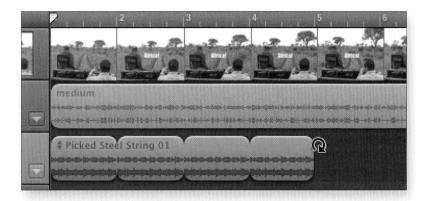

> **tip** If your movie has sound, you may want to mute it or lower its volume. To mute it, click the Mute button underneath the track name. To lower its volume, drag the track volume slider to the left (Figure 5.29).

Figure 5.29
Muting the movie's audio track

Adding more loops

1. In the Loop browser, click Picked Steel String 02. Not surprisingly, it sounds like it might go well with Picked Steel String 01.

2. Drag it to the timeline at the end of the Acoustic Guitar track, immediately following the last repetition of Picked Steel String 01.

3. Hit Return to go back to the beginning of the song and press Play. Now you're getting somewhere.

4. Click and drag a marquee around both guitar regions to select them (**Figure 5.30**).

Figure 5.30
Select both regions.

5. Chose Edit > Copy (or press Command-C) to copy both regions.

6. Click the 9 in the beat ruler to move the playhead to the end of the second region.

7. Choose Edit > Paste. You should now have four regions of acoustic guitar, ending at the beginning of measure 17.

8. Move the last region, Picked Steel String 02.1, ahead two measures, so it begins at measure 15. There should now be a two-measure gap between it and the previous region.

9. In the Loop browser, select Picked Steel String 04 and drag it to the timeline into the hole you just created. It should span from measures 13 through 15.

10. Hit Return and then press the spacebar to hear your song so far.

The loops Picked Steel String 01, 02, and 04 are all part of the same loop "family." Apple specifically designed loop families so you could mix and match them on a track and it would sound like a natural performance. Some especially nice loop families to check out are Delicate Piano, Emotional Piano, and Fusion Electric Piano, among others.

Add more instruments

Your project is starting to sound like a real song, but it definitely needs some other elements. In this next section, you're going to add some new instruments and start to flesh out the arrangement.

At the beginning of this section I said you were going to create a rock soundtrack, and nothing says "rock" like a good backbeat. It's time to add some drums.

1. In the Loop browser, click the Reset button to start a new search.

2. Click Kits to select all the drum-kit–related loops.

3. Now I'm going to show you a nifty trick you can use to audition new loops in the context of the rest of the song: Press Return and then the spacebar to begin playing the song from the beginning.

4. While the song is playing, click Classic Rock Beat 01 in the Loop browser.

   The drumbeat starts playing along with the guitar. There may be a slight delay before the drumbeat begins. This is so the beat starts at the beginning of a measure and allows the two loops to synchronize.

> **tip**
>
> **You can adjust the volume of the drum loop by moving the volume slider at the bottom of the Loop browser. You can also use the volume slider to the left of the acoustic guitar regions to adjust the volume of the guitar track.**

5. The beat works well with the guitar loops, but it might be nice to start with a fill. Drummers often play fills, which are sort of like mini-solos, in between musical phrases and at the beginnings of sections to add excitement and sustain listeners' interest.

6. Click Classic Rock Beat 03. The first half is similar to the earlier drum beat, but the second half features a nice fill that would work perfectly.

7. Drag Classic Rock Beat 03 into the timeline below the acoustic guitar track. Position it so it starts at measure 7.

> **note**
>
> **Notice that the drum track is green, while the guitar track is blue. This is because the guitar track is what GarageBand calls a Real Instrument track, which means that it's an actual audio recording of a guitar player. The drum track, by contrast, is a Software Instrument track. Instead of being an actual recording of a drum kit, it's a collection of instructions that trigger the computer to play samples—short recordings of individual drum hits that, combined together, sound like a real drum kit. One of the cool things about Software Instrument tracks is that you can actually edit the instructions and change the**

notes, or in this case the drum hits, that are being triggered. You can also change the instrument that's playing the notes—to a different drum kit or even to a piano or a cello.

8. I want to start with the fill, so cut the drum region in half and delete the first part. As in iMovie, you can split a region at the playhead. To do so, click the beat ruler at measure 8, and then select Edit > Split (Command-T) to split the region at the playhead.

9. Make sure that the first region is selected and press Delete.

10. Drag Classic Rock Beat 01 into the timeline immediately after the fill (**Figure 5.31**). Loop it one and a half times so it ends where the guitar does.

Figure 5.31
Replacing the region

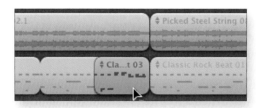

11. Listen to the song from the beginning. The drums add some activity and interest during the repeat of the guitar part.

Create a new section

Things are starting to come together, but where to go next? You could repeat the section again and add more instruments, but that could get boring. Adding music to your movie should make it *more* exciting, not less. Instead, consider switching gears and adding a new section.

Starting with a new loop

1. Reset the Loop browser and click Guitars.

2. Drag Picked Steel String 08 onto the Acoustic Guitar track at measure 19, at the end of the existing guitar regions.

3. Loop it three times so it ends at measure 27.

4. Reset the Loop browser and click the Kits button to return to the drum loops.

5. Drag Classic Rock Beat 01 into the Kits track at measure 19. Loop it once so it ends with the new guitar region.

6. Scroll to measure 8 and find the drum fill at the beginning of the drum track.

7. Hold down the Option key and drag the fill to measure 18 in the timeline. The fill replaces that measure of Classic Rock Beat 01.

 note Option-dragging copies a region, but GarageBand is finicky about holding down the Option key *before* you start to drag. If you do these two actions at once, you end up dragging the loop itself and not a copy.

Adding some bass

1. Reset the Loop browser again and click Bass to reveal the bass loops.

 2. Click the Cycle button to enable the cycle region. Watch the beat ruler while you click the button. A new bar appears under the beat ruler, with the same tick marks as the ruler. This is the cycle ruler.

   The cycle region enables you to audition one area of your song repeatedly. This makes it easier to find loops that work with a specific section or make small tweaks to a particular area of a song.

3. Click in the cycle ruler and drag from measure 19 to measure 27 (**Figure 5.32**). A yellow bar appears where you drag, defining the cycle region.

Figure 5.32
The cycle region

4. Press Play. GarageBand plays the cycled section of the song. When the playhead gets to the end of the cycle region, it jumps back to the beginning of the yellow bar.

5. With the cycle region still playing, click Rock Bass 01 in the Loop browser.

6. This bass part works perfectly with the new section of the song, so drag it into the timeline and loop it so it fills the cycle region.

At this point in the process, you've got several elements going at once, and the song may be getting loud. Yes, loud is often good when it comes to rock and roll, but there is a limit. Look at the master level meter (Figure 5.33). If you see red dots to the right of the meters, see the sidebar below.

Figure 5.33
Clipping indicators

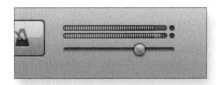

Set Your Levels

If you see red dots next to the master level meters, your song is too loud and your levels are *clipping*. Clipping is bad, because at extreme levels it results in harsh-sounding digital distortion, which sounds like bad radio static and can ruin an otherwise good song. Here's what you can do to avoid clipping:

1. Turn down the volume of your tracks. Use the track level sliders to turn down each individual track and find a balance between their relative levels. This is by far the best way to combat master level clipping. Don't be afraid to turn track volumes down considerably. You can always turn them up later if you need to.

2. Reset the clipping indicators. Click the red clipping indicators next to the master level meters to reset them. (This feature lets you tell at a glance that your song is clipping—you don't need to constantly watch the indicators.)

3. Turn down the master level. If you've turned down the individual tracks and reset the clipping indicators and your song is still clipping, you can always turn down the master level a hair as well. I'd actually recommend going back and adjusting the individual track levels some more and only using the master level slider as a last resort, but it's there if you need it.

Selecting some favorites

You're going to be using a lot of the same loops over and over again. It would be great if GarageBand had a way to select some favorite loops so you didn't have to keep hunting for the same loops in the Loop browser. Well guess what? It does!

1. Reset the Loop browser and click Guitars.

2. Find Picked Steel String 01 in the results list.

3. Click its checkbox in the Fav column (**Figure 5.34**).

Figure 5.34
Mark your favorites.

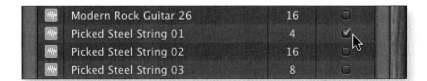

4. Do the same for the other loops in the song (Picked Steel String 02, 04, and 08; Classic Rock Beat 01; and Rock Bass 01 and 03).

5. Reset the Loop browser again and click Favorites. Voila! There are all your loops in one handy place!

Using the resize pointer

1. From the Favorites list, drag Picked Steel String 04 onto the end of the Acoustic Guitar track, followed by Picked Steel String 02.

   This transitional section should be four measures long, not six, so you'll need to crop the second loop.

2. Hover the pointer over the lower-right corner of the final guitar loop. A bracket with arrowheads appears, called the resize pointer.

3. Click and drag with the resize pointer to make the region two measures shorter (**Figure 5.35**). It should now end at measure 31.

Figure 5.35
Drag the resize pointer.

4. Drag Classic Rock Beat 01 onto the Kits track under the two new guitar regions.

Transposing a region

1. Drag Rock Bass 03 onto the Elec Bass track, under the new regions.

2. Use the resize pointer to shorten the new bass region to two measures.

3. Option-drag the shortened bass region to copy it and fill out the remainder of this new section.

4. Double-click the second new bass region to open it in the editor.

5. On the left-hand side of the editor, move the Pitch slider to 5 (**Figure 5.36**). This raises the pitch of the region by five semitones, the equivalent of five white and black keys on a piano.

Figure 5.36
Adjusting the pitch

 6. Click the editor button to close the editor.

Add a new instrument

The piece sounds great so far, but it's time for some new blood. This is supposed to be a rock song, so how about some electric guitar?

Finding some new guitar loops

1. Reset the Loop browser and click the Guitars button. I want to add some of the loops in the Edgy Rock Guitar family. Unfortunately, you'll notice that the only ones visible at the moment are Edgy Rock Guitar 01, 06, and 14. What happened to the others?

2. Open GarageBand's Preferences and click the Loops button.

3. Deselect the "Keyword Browsing: Filter for more relevant results" checkbox (**Figure 5.37**).

Figure 5.37
View more results by turning off filtering.

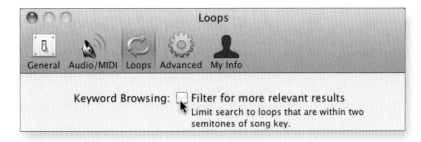

4. Close Preferences.

5. The Loop browser has reset itself, so click the Guitars button again.

6. Scroll down to the Edgy Rock Guitar family, and notice that all the loops, 01–15, show up in the results list now.

7. Favorite 01, 10, and 11.

Adding edgy rock guitar

1. Reset the Loop browser and click the Favorites button.

2. Drag Picked Steel String 01 onto the Acoustic Guitar track and loop it from measure 31 to 39.

3. Select the drum and bass regions between measures 19 and 27 (Classic Rock Beat 01 and Rock Bass 01).

4. Option-drag them to measure 31.

It may help to zoom out a bit to see more of the timeline. To do so, drag the zoom slider, at the bottom of the track header section (Figure 5.38). Dragging left zooms out, and dragging right zooms in.

Figure 5.38
The zoom slider

5. Drag Edgy Rock Guitar 10 into the timeline underneath the Elec Bass track.

6. Loop it once so it ends at measure 39 with the rest of the regions.

Finish your song

It's time to finish this puppy. You're going to copy and paste a few sections, add a couple more guitar parts, and fade the piece out.

Copying sections

1. Select all the regions between measures 27 and 31 (the section with the transposed bass region).

2. Option-drag them to measure 39.

3. Select all the regions between measures 19 and 27, with Picked Steel String 08, and Option-drag them to measure 43.

4. Finally, select all the regions between measures 31 and 39, with Edgy Rock Guitar 10, and drag them to measure 51.

5. Copy them one more time and drop them at measure 59.

Adding the final guitar parts and finishing your soundtrack

1. In the Favorites section of the Loop browser, find Edgy Rock Guitar 01 and drag it to the timeline at measure 39, under the existing Elec Guitar track (**Figure 5.39**).

Figure 5.39
Dragging a new guitar loop

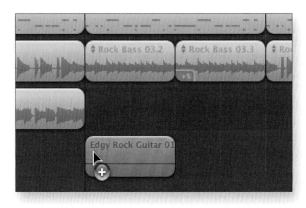

 You could add the new loop to the existing electric guitar track, but Edgy Rock Guitar 01 is quieter than 10, and for now, it's easier to leave them on their own tracks to adjust their relative volumes.

2. Drag Edgy Rock Guitar 11 onto the first electric guitar track at measure 59, over the existing region that's there. As with the drum fill earlier, it will replace the guitar region that's there.

3. Loop Edgy Rock Guitar 11 once so it ends with the rest of the regions. Again, it replaces the guitar region that was there.

4. Listen to the song all the way through once or twice, making sure everything sounds balanced and even. Use the track volume sliders to adjust track volumes, and make sure your master level meters aren't clipping. If they are, see the sidebar "Set Your Levels," earlier.

    Also check to make sure the movie sound is at an appropriate level. If there's dialogue in your video that you want to be audible, you'll need to turn the music down quite a bit.

5. Select Track > Fade Out to create a fade at the end of the piece, which is implemented on the Master Volume control (**Figure 5.40**).

Figure 5.40
Fade out at the end
of the song.

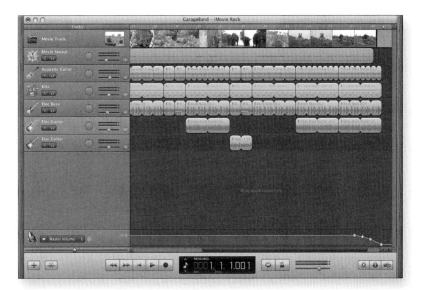

Fade Out uses the last region in the song to determine where the fade-out ends. If your movie contains audio and is significantly longer than the song, the song won't fade, only the movie sound will. To remedy this, do one of the following: Copy one or more sections of the song to make it longer; or, delete the Movie Sound track. You're not going to use it until you reopen your video in iMovie anyway, so it's unnecessary at the moment.

Exporting your song

1. Use the scroll bar at the bottom of the timeline to scroll to the end of the song.

2. Find the end-of-project marker in the beat ruler (**Figure 5.41**).

Figure 5.41
Setting the important end-of-project marker

3. Move the end-of-project marker to the end of the last region in your song. This sets the total length of your song and determines where GarageBand ends its export.

4. Click the Mute button in the Movie Sound track.

5. Open GarageBand Preferences and mark the Audio Preview checkbox (if it isn't already checked). Close Preferences.

6. Save and close your song. GarageBand exports the audio and creates an iLife preview, which you'll use in a moment when you reopen the song in iMovie.

 In this case, you're going to bring your song back into iMovie and export the movie from there. But you also have the option of exporting directly from GarageBand. To do so, select Share > Export Movie to Disk before you mute the Movie Sound track.

Finishing your film in iMovie

1. In iMovie, open your video project.

2. Click the Music and Sound Effects button.

3. Find your GarageBand folder in the Music and Sound Effects pop-up menu. Browse to find your song.

4. Drag the song to the Project browser so that it's added as a background audio track.

Your song is now part of your iMovie project. The green area indicates the length of your song. If your movie is longer or shorter than your song, you can edit the movie to fit. You can also edit it so important cuts in your film happen in sync with musical changes. This makes it feel like the music "fits" your movie better.

Now pour yourself a cold beverage and relax in a comfy chair. You've just created your first GarageBand song! You can now use these techniques to create all kinds of great music using just the loops that come with GarageBand.

6

Share Your Movies

Now that you've put time into crafting a great movie, don't let it languish unseen on your hard drive. Set it free! iMovie makes it easy to share your movies with friends, family, and even total strangers (the latter via the Web, of course—I don't expect you to hand out DVDs to random people on the street, but I suppose nothing is stopping you).

In this chapter, I walk you through the steps to share your movies on DVD; on the Web; on the iPad, iPhone, and iPod touch; and on a big-screen television using the second-generation Apple TV.

Make a DVD Project

Difficulty: Easy

Software needed: iDVD

There are now more ways than ever to view movies—computers, phones, iPads, even gaming devices—but most people still prefer DVDs. The shiny discs are also nearly ubiquitous: Most people have a DVD player or some other DVD-capable device. You can hand someone a disc and not have to worry about download speeds, resolution, file sizes, or any other potential pitfalls of various sharing methods.

In this project, I'm going to show you how to bring a movie into iDVD, create gorgeous menus, and burn a disc, all quicker than you can say Francis Ford Coppola.

 iDVD creates standard-definition DVDs, not high-definition Blu-ray discs. That means any HD footage will be downsampled to SD resolution. To display HD video, look into sharing via the Web or an Apple TV.

Prepare your project for iDVD

One feature of DVDs is the capability to jump to specific scenes within a movie. When you set up chapter markers in iMovie and then export the project, iDVD correctly translates the markers into chapters.

Setting chapter markers

1. Make sure Show Advanced Tools is enabled in iMovie's preferences (otherwise, the marker icons don't appear).

2. Drag the Chapter Marker icon to a location in your project (**Figure 6.1**). You can also Control-click (or right-click) a frame and choose Add Chapter Marker from the contextual menu.

3. Enter a name for the chapter and press Return.

 When dragging the Chapter Marker icon, you can't add chapters during transitions. But when using the contextual menu, you can.

> **tip**
>
> Chapter markers are rust colored, with an arrow before the name. Comment markers, on the other hand, are brown. Comment markers are used for your own organization; they appear only in the Project browser and aren't exported with the project.

Figure 6.1
Creating a
chapter marker

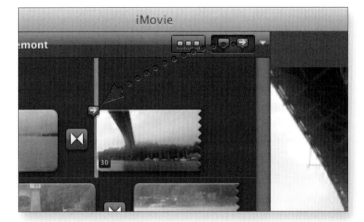

Once you've created markers, you can edit them in several ways:

* To move a marker, click it and drag it to a new location.

* To delete a marker, select it and press Delete.

* To jump to a chapter, click the disclosure triangle to the right of the marker icons and select the chapter name from the pop-up menu (**Figure 6.2**).

Figure 6.2
Jump to a
chapter marker.

Sharing to iDVD

This step is easy: Choose Share > iDVD. iMovie prepares your project and opens it in iDVD, launching the app if necessary.

Make sure you have 10–20 GB of free hard disk space before creating a project in iDVD. Authoring a DVD requires a lot of hard disk headroom.

Choose a theme in iDVD

Every screen in a DVD is referred to as a *menu*, and every menu must have a theme. Themes are both wallpaper and roadmap—they dress up the various navigation pages and give your disc style, but they also provide valuable navigation assistance. As one might expect from a design-focused company like Apple, iDVD includes several attractive themes to choose from.

When iMovie hands its project over to iDVD, a theme is already applied—either the first theme in the list or the one that was active the last time you used iDVD. However, you can change it at any time.

Choosing a theme in iDVD

1. Click the Themes button to display the Themes pane, if it isn't already visible.

2. Scroll through the list of themes to find one you like. Don't forget to check the pop-up menu at the top of the pane to access older iDVD themes (**Figure 6.3**).

Figure 6.3
Accessing older themes

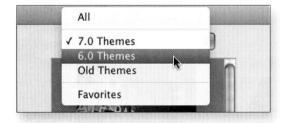

3. Click a theme to select it. If you're working in Standard (4:3) aspect ratio, iDVD offers to switch to Widescreen (16:9) mode. Click Keep to leave the mode unchanged (unless you do want to switch).

You may also see a dialog asking if you want to apply the same theme to all the submenus attached to the current project. Click OK. After a few moments, the theme changes in the main window.

 Some themes have animated menus and buttons. To preview your chosen theme in motion, click the Motion button (Figure 6.4). You can also scrub the playhead to any point in the animation.

Figure 6.4
Previewing motion

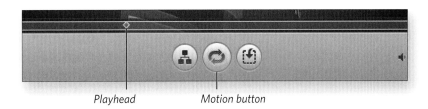

Playhead   Motion button

Edit theme elements

Most of iDVD's themes include plenty of areas where you can customize the appearance to tie in your own content. Text labels for titles and menus are editable; you can add photos and videos to drop zones to preview the disc's content; and you can change the background music that plays while the person viewing the disc chooses which menu items to select.

Editing title and menu text

1. Click the text you want to edit, and then click it again to select the text. Don't *double-click* it—depending on the text, that may play the movie or take you to a submenu.

2. Enter your text (**Figure 6.5**). Hit Enter or Return to break the line.

Figure 6.5
Editing text

3. Click outside the text field to apply your changes.

> **tip** You can also add new text anywhere on the screen. Choose Project > Add Text, or press Command-K. To remove text, select it and press the Delete key.

Adding drop zone items

1. Click the Media button to display the Media pane.

2. Click the Photos or Movies button at the top of the pane to reveal your iPhoto, Aperture, or Photo Booth libraries, as well as everything in iMovie (including all of the Event footage).

3. Drag a movie, a photo, or multiple photos to a drop zone in the main window, indicated by a yellow border (**Figure 6.6**). Alternatively, drag photos or movies from the Finder as well.

Figure 6.6
Add movies or photos to drop zones.

> **note** For themes that include several drop zones, it's easier to use the Drop Zones Editor. Click the Edit Drop Zones button to display the editor. Then, drag media into one of the indicated zones (Figure 6.7).

Figure 6.7
The Drop Zones Editor

Edit Drop Zones button

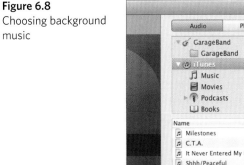

tip So far I've talked only about the main menu, but a DVD can have submenus as well. If you added chapter markers in iMovie, you automatically get a Scene Selection button. Double-click the button to view its submenu, where you can choose a theme and edit its titles, drop zones, and other elements.

Adding background music

Some iDVD themes come with music already in place, and others are silent. Either way, you can add your own music using the Media pane.

1. Switch to the Media pane and click the Audio button.

2. Locate an audio file you want to use. The browser lets you choose files from your iTunes and GarageBand libraries. To narrow your search, select a playlist from the upper part of the pane, or enter a song or artist name in the search field at the bottom (**Figure 6.8**).

   Click the Play button to preview your selection.

Figure 6.8
Choosing background music

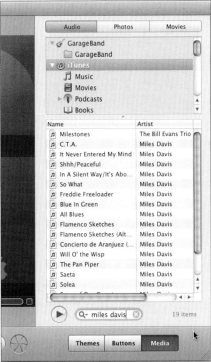

3. Click the Show Inspector button to bring up the inspector.

4. Drag your selection to the audio well (**Figure 6.9**). Set the volume level using the slider under the audio well.

Figure 6.9
Specify background music using the inspector.

Burn your project to disc

When you're happy with how your menus look, you're ready to finalize your project and burn it to a disc.

Previewing the project

Preview your project by clicking the Play button. iDVD shows you how the final project will appear, including menus and music. Test the navigation and playback using the virtual remote to make sure everything works the way you want it to.

Burning the disc

1. Choose Project > Project Info. Here you can change the disc name, the video mode (NTSC or PAL), and the quality at which the project will be encoded (**Figure 6.10**). The qualities vary as follows:

- **Best Performance:** For projects that contain less than 60 minutes of video, Best Performance offers speedier burn times and the capability to encode materials in the background while you work.

- **High Quality:** When your project exceeds 60 minutes, or you want to guarantee higher-quality encoding than Best Performance, this option is available.

- **Professional Quality:** If you're willing to wait as much as three times the time it takes to burn a disc in High Quality mode, Professional Quality gives you the highest caliber disc, featuring richer colors and better reproduction.

Figure 6.10
The important Project Info window

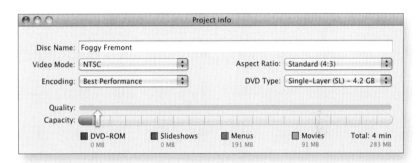

> The capacity estimate in the Project Info window is based on the quality setting you choose. If you've chosen Best Performance and your project won't fit on a disc, switch to High or Professional Quality (which utilize better compression at the expense of speed) and note how the capacity estimate changes.

2. When you're happy with the disc settings, close the Project Info window.

3. Insert a blank DVD.

 4. Click the Burn button. iDVD processes all of your project's assets and burns a disc. Depending on the quality setting you chose, this can take a *long* time (sometimes more than four hours), so it makes sense to burn your discs when you're not waiting to use your computer for something else.

> After burning a disc, make sure to test it in your DVD player before sending it out into the world. If it's an important disc, test it in numerous devices, just to be sure.

Learn All about iDVD

Although iDVD is included in the boxed version of iLife '11, Apple hasn't actually updated the software in any significant way since 2008. It still works—Apple just believes that the future is in sharing, not shiny discs. I covered iDVD in depth in my book *iMovie '08 and iDVD '08 for Mac OS X: Visual QuickStart Guide*, and for the iMovie '09 release, I made the entire iDVD portion of that book available as a free, downloadable PDF.

The PDF includes everything you want to know about iDVD in detail: adding movies, building photo slideshows, customizing menu screens, working with drop zones, and much more that I didn't have room to cover in this book. If you have any interest at all in creating DVDs, go get it at www.jeffcarlson.com/idvd/.

Share a Movie on the Web

Difficulty: Easy

Software needed: Web browser, iWeb

It wasn't too long ago that streaming full-length movies on the Web seemed like a distant dream, but now it's commonplace (roughly one-fifth of all Internet traffic during peak hours belongs to the video-sharing site Netflix). Whether you've edited an epic masterpiece or just a short slice-of-life movie, it's easy to share your own video using sites like MobileMe, YouTube, Vimeo, Facebook, and Flickr. If you prefer to host a movie on your own site, iWeb makes that just as easy.

Share to MobileMe Gallery

Apple's MobileMe service includes features such as synchronizing data between multiple Macs and iOS devices, email, and sharing photos and videos using the MobileMe Gallery. If you have a MobileMe account, here's how to make your movie available online.

Sharing to MobileMe Gallery

1. In iMovie, choose Share > MobileMe Gallery. The Share window appears (**Figure 6.11**).

Figure 6.11
MobileMe Gallery sharing options

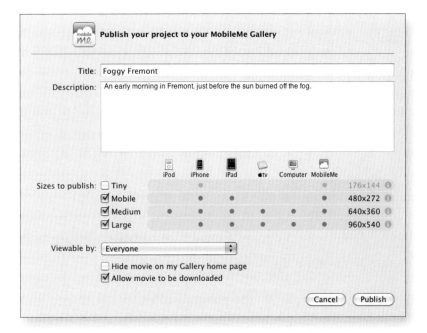

2. The name of your project appears in the Title field, but you can change it here if you like. Also, feel free to add an optional description in the next field.

3. Mark the checkboxes next to the sizes you wish to upload. Sharing multiple sizes ensures that viewers with varying broadband speeds can view the movie. However, note that the largest size MobileMe supports is 960 x 540, not HD.

4. From the "Viewable by" pop-up menu, choose whether to restrict access to the movie. Options include:

   • **Everyone.** The video is not restricted.

   • **Only me.** The video appears only for you when you're logged into MobileMe in a Web browser.

   • **Edit names and passwords.** You can require that a visitor enters a name and password to view the movie; for example, if you want someone to review an unfinished draft of the movie without making it public.

To create a new login, choose this option. In the dialog that appears, click the + button and enter a new name and password combination (**Figure 6.12**). Lastly, click OK and then choose that login from the pop-up menu.

Figure 6.12
Creating names and passwords

5. To further mask a video's existence, enable the "Hide movie on my Gallery home page" checkbox. With this option on, you need to send a direct link to the movie to people with whom you want to share it.

6. If you want people to be able to save a copy of the movie for them-selves, enable the "Allow movie to be downloaded" checkbox.

7. Click the Publish button. iMovie prepares the versions you specified and uploads them. When that's complete, a dialog appears with options to view the movie or share its location.

Share to YouTube, Facebook, Vimeo, or CNN iReport

We've all watched something on YouTube, the ubiquitous online video site. And many of us secretly (or not so secretly) want one of our videos to go viral so we can bask in our 15 minutes in the spotlight. iMovie includes the ability to share directly to YouTube, Facebook, Vimeo, and CNN iReport. The following steps assume you already have an account at one of the services. I'm using YouTube as the example, but the options for each service are similar.

Sharing to YouTube, Facebook, Vimeo, or CNN iReport

1. In iMovie, choose Share and then the name of the service.

2. In the Share window that appears, enter your account name and password (**Figure 6.13**).

Figure 6.13
Sharing to YouTube

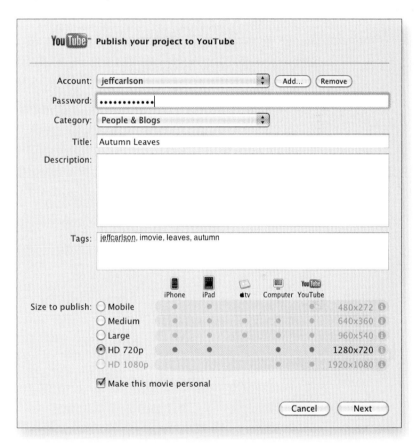

3. Choose a category. This determines where your video will appear under the Browse tab at the top of each page.

4. Enter a title and description for your video.

5. Enter descriptive tags to help viewers find your video when searching. For example, if your video is of you giving a soufflé baking

demonstration, you might enter "soufflé," "cooking," "baking," and "French."

6. Choose a size. Depending on the size of your original video, some sizes may be disabled. Larger sizes naturally take longer to upload.

7. If you'd like your video to be public and viewable by anyone, uncheck "Make this movie personal."

   For uploading to Facebook or Vimeo, change the privacy setting by choosing an option from the "Viewable by" pop-up menu.

8. Click Next. The terms of service appear, essentially telling you not to upload content that doesn't belong to you.

9. Click Publish to upload your video.

Once the video has been uploaded, a dialog comes up giving you the option of notifying a friend or opening the movie. It may take some time before the video is publicly available, however, because the service needs to optimize the content for viewing.

Export and share to Flickr

Since 2008, popular photo-sharing site Flickr has been hosting video as well, albeit in a more limited way than YouTube and Vimeo. Although iMovie provides no direct route to send video to Flickr, all you have to do is export the movie as a file you can upload separately. Flickr videos are limited to 90 seconds and 150 MB, so if you're looking to share a 20-minute movie on extreme quilting, look to one of the other options.

Exporting video from iMovie

1. Choose Share > Export Movie, or press Command-E.

2. In the Share window, select a name for your video and choose a location on your hard drive. For lack of a better option, the default Movies folder often serves as a good spot.

3. Choose a size. If some of the options are grayed out, that means your original footage doesn't support those sizes.

4. Click Export. iMovie compresses the video and saves it to your hard drive.

If you hover your mouse over the "i" next to the movie dimensions, you can see more info about the chosen output resolution (Figure 6.14). Specifically, it shows you the compression scheme used, the number of frames per second (fps), the data rate of the movie, and the size of the resulting file in megabytes.

Figure 6.14
Preview export settings and estimated file size.

Uploading the video to Flickr

1. In a Web browser, navigate to www.flickr.com.

2. Log in to your Flickr or Yahoo account. Your Flickr home page opens.

3. Click the Upload Photos & Video link.

4. Click Choose Photos and Videos, and locate the movie file you exported in the previous steps.

5. Select a privacy setting.

6. Click Upload Photos and Videos. Flickr shows the progress as your video uploads and lets you know when it's done.

7. If you'd like to add your video to a set or add a description or tags, click the Add a Description link. If not, you're done!

Navigate to your photostream to see your video in all its Flickr-y glory. Click the video to view it at full size.

Share to iWeb

If you're like most people, you don't want to become an HTML expert in order to create your Web site. Apple knows this, and they designed iWeb to make it easy to create a beautiful, fun, dynamic site that doesn't require months of sleepless nights reading HTML and JavaScript text-books. Creating a simple site and sharing it on iWeb is a snap.

Opening iWeb

1. Once you've finished your video in iMovie, select Share > Media Browser. This lets iWeb use your iMovie project file to create an appropriately formatted movie you can stream from your site.

2. Launch iWeb.

3. In the MobileMe dialog that opens, you can sign in to your account, learn more about the service, or say no thanks and continue to iWeb. (You can also check the "Don't show again" checkbox to avoid seeing this dialog in the future.)

4. If you haven't used iWeb before, the next window that greets you is the Getting Started video. Click to play it if you're interested, other-wise close the window. The video gives you a quick overview of iWeb and how it works. If you've never played with iWeb before, it's an informative four minutes.

 If you look carefully, you'll notice that the welcome video talks about iWeb '09. What happened to iWeb '11? Well, they're the same applica-tion—Apple hasn't released anything but maintenance updates since iLife '09 came out.

5. iWeb prompts you to pick a template to begin your site (**Figure 6.15**). Choose a theme from the list on the left. You get a lot of options—from fun and informal, to hip and modern, to themed looks like Road Trip and Comic Book.

6. Choose a page template from the list on the right. Since you're making a movie page, choose Movie.

Figure 6.15
Choosing an iWeb template

Fine Line

Goldenrod

Modern Frame

My Albums   Movie   Blog

7. Click the Choose button. iWeb opens your page in the main window.

> **note** You can always change your theme later, and iWeb will instantly swap out all of the visual assets of your page. The only catch is that you have to change themes one page at a time, so this could become tedious if you have a large site.

Adding content to your site

1. If the Media browser isn't already visible, click the Show Media button.

2. Click the Movies tab at the top of the browser.

3. Locate your movie and drag it to the placeholder on the page (**Figure 6.16**).

Figure 6.16
Adding a movie to a placeholder

Africa   2:10   Foggy Fremont   1:38

My First Project   0:30   20101013-MVI_...   0:22

20101013-MVI_...   0:22   20101013-MVI_...   1:17

4. Click the movie to select it.

5. If the inspector is not already visible, click the Inspector button.

6. Click the QuickTime button in the inspector.

7. Change any of the options for your movie (**Figure 6.17**):

Figure 6.17
QuickTime controls
in the inspector

- **Start and Stop:** If you want only a portion of the movie to play, use the left slider to change the start point and the right slider to change the end point.

- **Poster Frame:** Drag the slider to choose the frame that's displayed when the page first loads.

- **Autoplay:** Check this box to make the movie play automatically when the page loads.

- **Loop:** Check this box to make the movie play repeatedly.

- **Show movie controller:** Displays the QuickTime controls at the bottom of the movie. If you deselect this checkbox and disable Autoplay, visitors can play the movie by double-clicking it.

8. To change the page's placeholder text, double-click a text box (**Figure 6.18**).

Figure 6.18
Change the
placeholder text
(unless you want to
impress people with
your Latin).

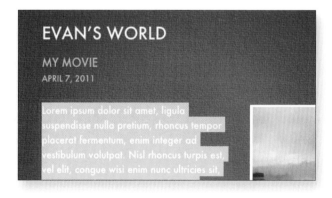

9. To rename the page from the default "Movie," double-click the name in iWeb's sidebar on the left and type a new title.

 Learn more about creating and customizing an entire site with iWeb by reading my colleague Steve Sande's ebook, *Take Control of iWeb '09* (www.takecontrolbooks.com/iweb).

Publishing your site with MobileMe

You've created a page, but nobody else can see it until you publish it online. To do that, you have two options, MobileMe or FTP. (I don't cover the third option, Local Folder, because it's less popular and more difficult to set up than the other two.)

A MobileMe site is great because it's easy to set up and can be password protected. The only catch, aside from needing a MobileMe account, is that you can't run a commercial Web site on MobileMe. Here's how to set up a MobileMe site:

1. Click the site's name in iWeb's sidebar. (If you haven't changed it yet, it will be labeled with its default name, "Site" (**Figure 6.19**).

Figure 6.19
Setting up MobileMe publishing

2. Choose MobileMe from the "Publish to" pop-up menu.

3. Enter a site name and your contact email; both are optional. If you are publishing more than one site on your MobileMe account, the site name shows up in the URL. If you don't choose a site name, MobileMe automatically assigns "Site 2," "Site 3," and so on.

    Your email address is only used if you have a contact link on the site.

4. If you want to make your site private, mark the "Make my published site private" checkbox and enter password information.

 5. Click the Publish Site button to upload the files and take the site live.

Publishing your site via FTP

If you're not a MobileMe user, or you'd rather publish your site to a third-party Web host, then FTP (File Transfer Protocol) may be your best bet. Plenty of hosts out there offer their services for $10 a month or less. Assuming that you've already signed up with a Web host and have FTP settings at hand, here's how to publish your iWeb site using FTP.

1. Click the site's name in the sidebar.

2. From the "Publish to" pop-up menu, choose FTP Server.

3. Enter a site name and your contact email; both are optional. The site name is used to name the folder that stores all your site files. Your email address is only used if you have a contact link on the Web site.

4. Enter the FTP Server settings. This is information you should have gotten from your Web host, including the server address to use, your username and login, the directory path, and which protocol to use. If you have questions about any of these, contact your Web host.

 iWeb has somewhat peculiar requirements about the server address and directory path. In the case of the server address, leave off the initial "ftp.". For example, if your host said to use "ftp.myhost.com" as the server address, use "myhost.com" in iWeb. For the directory path, leave off the initial "/", so "/mywebfolder" should be entered as "mywebfolder".

5. Click the Test Connection button to check your settings.

6. Enter the URL of your site. This is the root-level URL of your Web site (for example, www.example.com). This is required.

 7. Click the Publish Site button to upload the files and take the site live. iWeb displays a warning about uploading copyrighted content (you did create all the content yourself, didn't you?).

8. Click Continue. iWeb prepares the files for uploading and then informs you that publishing will continue in the background. Once again, click Continue.

   When the site has been uploaded, iWeb announces the fact and gives you the option to announce the site in an email or to visit it.

Share a Movie on iTunes, iOS Devices, and the Apple TV

Difficulty: Easy

Software needed: iTunes

Hardware needed: iPad, iPhone, iPod touch, or Apple TV

DVDs and the Web aren't the only ways you can share your movies. I carry home movies on my iPad and iPhone, store them in iTunes, and watch them on my HDTV using the second-generation Apple TV. The iPad in particular is a beautiful and impressive way to show off video if you need a portable presentation device.

Share your movie to iTunes

The first step to getting your video onto any of these devices is to get it into iTunes. Fortunately, since iTunes is the hub for all iOS devices, iMovie makes that a breeze.

Sharing your movie to iTunes

1. Select Share > iTunes.

2. Choose a size based on your movie's final destination (**Figure 6.20**). Medium resolution is the only size that works on all devices, so that's a good option when in doubt.

   However, if you own an iPhone 4 or fourth-generation iPod touch, stick with the higher-resolution options, since their Retina Display screens can support the larger sizes.

Figure 6.20
Publishing to iTunes

tip

The sharing dialog for iTunes hasn't been updated to reflect that the Apple TV now looks different (black instead of silver) and can accommodate HD 720p video. Hopefully this will be fixed in a future iMovie update.

3. Click the Publish button. A dialog appears showing you iMovie's progress. When it's finished, iTunes opens.

4. In the sidebar, click Movies to reveal the video in your iTunes library.

Synchronize with iOS devices

Now that your movie is in iTunes, it's easy to sync it with your iPad, iPhone, or iPod.

Synchronizing with iOS devices

1. Connect your iOS device. It appears in the iTunes sidebar, under Devices.

2. Click the device's name to show its sync options (**Figure 6.21**).

Figure 6.21
An iPhone connected to the Mac

3. Click the Movies tab along the top of the main window.

4. Mark the Sync Movies checkbox. iMovie gives you the option of automatically syncing all your movies, automatically selecting certain movies, or specifying which movies you want to sync.

5. Check an automatic option or select specific movies (**Figure 6.22**).

6. Click Apply. iTunes begins the sync process. When it's finished you can eject your device and take your movie with you!

Figure 6.22
Movies chosen
manually for syncing

Watch a movie on the Apple TV

You may believe that your movie belongs on the big screen—but just how big? With a high-definition television and an Apple TV, you can stream your movie from iTunes or a recent iOS device onto the TV's large screen.

Make sure the Apple TV and the device containing the video are on the same network, and that they're both using Home Sharing:

- In iTunes, choose Advanced > Turn On Home Sharing and enter your Apple ID (the one you use to purchase items from the iTunes Store).

- On the Apple TV, choose Computers > Turn On Home Sharing and enter your Apple ID.

- On an iPad, iPhone, or iPod touch, go to Settings > iPod and enter your Apple ID under Home Sharing.

 In this section, I'm talking specifically about the second-generation Apple TV, the small black device. If you own a first-generation Apple TV (the larger, silver-and-gray model), you can sync movies to it in the same way as you do an iPhone, iPad, or iPod. The second-generation unit contains no internal hard disk, so all content is streamed to it.

Playing a movie using iTunes

1. In iTunes, start playing a movie.

2. Click the AirPlay button in the movie's controls and choose your Apple TV.

You can also set the Apple TV as the playback destination before you begin playing a movie. Click the AirPlay button at the lower-right corner of the iTunes window and choose the name of your Apple TV (Figure 6.23).

Figure 6.23
Choosing the
Apple TV in iTunes

Playing a movie from an Apple TV

1. Using the Apple TV's navigation, go to Computers > [name of the computer where your movie is located].

2. Choose Movies.

3. Scroll through the list of movies until you find the one you want, and then press the Select button on the remote to begin playing.

Playing a movie from an iOS device

1. Open the Videos app (or the iPod app, on an iPhone).

2. Locate your movie and start playing it.

3. Tap the AirPlay button and choose the name of your Apple TV (**Figure 6.24**).

Figure 6.24
Sending a movie to an
Apple TV from an iPad

7

Edit Video on the iPad, iPhone, or iPod touch

One of the hallmark characteristics of iMovie is that it enables anyone to quickly and easily edit a movie using various snippets of video they've shot. Now that Apple's mobile iOS devices all capture HD video, it makes sense that there should be a way to edit that footage together without waiting to bring it back to your computer.

iMovie for iOS takes the concepts used by the Mac version and makes them work on a mobile device. Although you won't find every feature from the desktop software, iMovie for iOS is more than capable of creating high-quality movies wherever you happen to have some video clips, an iOS device, and a bit of spare time.

Work with Projects in iMovie for iOS

To accommodate smaller screens compared to the Mac, and to take advantage of a touch interface, Apple made some significant design decisions when developing the mobile version of iMovie. Although most of it will be immediately familiar, there are some aspects—such as how iMovie organizes projects or handles themes—that may require some getting used to.

 iMovie for iOS is a separate $4.99 app available from the App Store. If you purchased the original version of the software, which ran on the iPhone 4 and fourth-generation iPod touch, you can upgrade to the latest version for free. Check for updates in the App Store app on your device or within iTunes on your computer.

 In addition to working on the iPhone 4 and fourth-generation iPod touch (the current models at the time of this writing), iMovie for iOS runs on the iPad 2—but not on the original iPad.

Create a new project

Every movie you edit is its own iMovie project, accessible from the neon-lit opening screen. To get you started quickly, however, iMovie jumps right into the editing environment after you create a new project. You can return later to grace the project with a name.

Creating a new project

 At the main screen, tap the New Project button. iMovie takes you to the editing environment. The interface differs between the iPad (**Figure 7.1**) and the iPhone or iPod touch (**Figure 7.2**) due to the sizes of the devices' screens. Each device enables you to edit in either the horizontal or portrait orientation.

 It's not currently possible to move projects between iMovie '11 and iMovie for iOS. Files created in the iPad version of iMovie's sister app GarageBand can currently be brought into GarageBand on the Mac, so

I'm optimistic that we'll see this capability arrive with iMovie in the future. (Although you can move projects between iOS devices, as I describe near the end of this chapter.)

Figure 7.1
The iPad editing environment in landscape orientation.

When viewed in portrait orientation, the Media bin is hidden and accessible as a popover window.

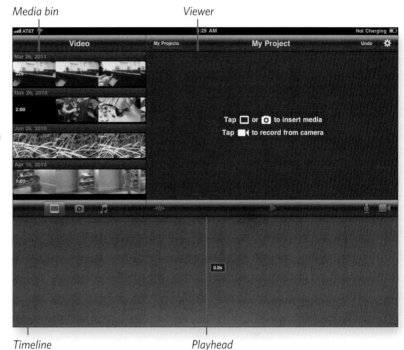

Figure 7.2
The iPhone and iPod touch editing environment

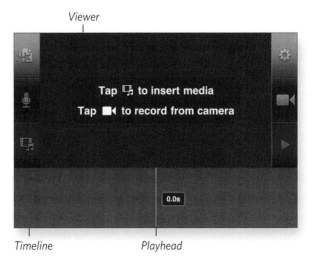

Naming your project

1. Make any edit, such as adding a clip to the timeline.

2. Tap the My Projects button to return to the opening screen.

3. Tap the title in the marquee to make it editable (**Figure 7.3**).

4. Enter a new title, and then tap the Done button on the virtual keyboard.

 If you create a project and then immediately return to the opening screen, iMovie discards the new project because it has no content.

Figure 7.3
Editing a project title

Choose the theme

Every movie must have a theme, even if you don't plan to use theme elements. New projects adopt the Modern theme, but you won't see evidence of it unless you specifically choose a theme transition or add a title to a clip. You can change a project's theme at any time. Any themed assets in the movie automatically switch to the chosen theme (which also means you can't mix and match elements from different themes in the same project).

Choosing the theme

1. Tap the Project Settings button.

2. In the Project Settings window, drag the theme thumbnails left or right to highlight the theme you want to use (**Figure 7.4**).

3. Tap outside the window to apply the setting; on the iPhone or iPod touch, tap the Done button.

Figure 7.4
Changing the theme

Apply a fade in or fade out to the movie

Instead of starting with the first frame of the first clip, you may want to begin your movie with a fade in from black. The Project Settings window includes a single-switch option for adding fades to the start and end of a project.

Applying a fade in or fade out

1. Tap the Project Settings button to open the Project Settings window.

2. Tap the switch next to "Fade in from black" or "Fade out to black" (or both) to change the setting from Off to On.

3. Tap outside the window or tap the Done button to apply the setting.

Open an existing project

iMovie keeps track of your saved projects on the opening screen, like you're choosing a video at a stylish multiplex. (Being from Seattle, I keep expecting a light drizzle of rain to come down while I'm scrolling through project thumbnails; maybe in a future update.)

Opening other projects

1. Tap the My Projects button (which displays the words on the iPad, and an icon, shown here, on the iPhone and iPod touch) to return to the main screen.

2. Swipe the project icons until the one you want is highlighted.

3. Tap the icon to open the project.

Add Video to a project

iMovie for iOS is pretty picky about the video it uses. Basically, if the video came from an iPad, iPhone, or iPod touch, you're golden. I've also had success with footage from my Flip MinoHD. If you want to bring in video you've shot using other cameras, you need to first convert it on your Mac. That said, there are several ways to get video into iMovie.

Capture video directly

Using the cameras on the device, you can record video directly into your iMovie timeline. With a project open, do the following.

Capturing video into iMovie

1. Tap the Camera button.

2. Set the mode switch to video (or to photo, if you want to capture a still photo).

3. Tap the Record button to begin capturing the footage (**Figure 7.5**).

4. Tap the Record button again to stop recording.

5. Press the Play button that appears to review your footage; you can also skim through the clip at the top of the screen.

Figure 7.5
Camera controls

Record   Photo/Video switch

6. If the clip is acceptable, tap the Use button. The video clip appears in the Video browser as well as at the point in your movie where the playhead was positioned before recording.

If not, tap the Retake button and shoot again.

Moving clips to the Camera Roll

 Video shot by the device stays with the project in which it was captured. It isn't automatically added to the Camera Roll, which is where the iOS stores photos and videos that have been shot by the device or, on the iPad, imported using the iPad Camera Connection Kit. To move a clip to the Camera Roll, tap the Edit button and then tap the Move button.

 Whenever possible, I prefer to shoot video using the Camera app instead of using iMovie. Shooting in iMovie makes the clips unavailable for other projects without moving them to the Camera Roll.

Import from a camera, iPhone, or iPod touch

If you own an iPad as well as an iPhone or iPod touch, you can import media to the iPad's Camera Roll using Apple's $29 iPad Camera Connection Kit. I'm far more likely to shoot video using my iPhone than my iPad 2, but I prefer to edit in iMovie on the iPad's larger screen when possible.

Importing from a camera, iPhone, or iPod touch

1. Connect the USB adapter from the iPad Camera Connection Kit to the iPad's sync port.

2. Plug the iPad's connector cable into the USB port on the adapter and the port of the iPhone or iPod touch.

3. Wake up both devices; the Photos app launches on the iPad, displaying the photos and videos on the iPhone or iPod touch.

4. Tap the videos and photos you wish to add; a blue checkmark indicates they're queued for importing (**Figure 7.6**).

5. Tap the Import button, and in the popover that appears, tap Import Selected to copy them to the Camera Roll.

6. When you're asked whether you want to delete or keep the imported photos on the iPhone or iPod touch, I recommend tapping Keep.

Figure 7.6
Video clips ready
to be imported

Add clips from the Media Library

With a library of clips to work from, it's easy to add clips to your project's timeline.

Adding clips from the Media Library

1. Scroll to the position in the timeline where you want the clip to appear. (This doesn't apply if no clips are in the timeline yet.)

 2. If you're editing on an iPhone or iPod touch, or you're holding the iPad in its portrait orientation, tap the Media Library button. (If editing on the iPad in landscape orientation, the Media Library appears in the upper-left corner.)

3. To preview the contents of a clip, drag your finger across it. The preview doesn't play in real time or with sound—the speed depends on how fast you drag your finger.

4. Tap once on a clip to reveal its selection handles.

5. Drag the handles to define which portion of the clip you want to add (**Figure 7.7**).

6. Tap the clip again to add it to the timeline.

Figure 7.7
Selecting a portion of a video clip to add

 A clip can be added only before or after an existing clip; you can't insert a new clip in the middle of an existing clip. To do that, you must first split the clip in the timeline (see "Splitting a clip," later in the chapter).

Edit Video

Working with video clips in the timeline is quite similar to editing clips in iMovie '11, but designed to be done with the tip of a finger instead of a mouse and keyboard, of course.

Play and skim video

 Unlike iMovie '11 (unless you're using the Single-Row View described in Chapter 2), the timeline in iMovie for iOS runs left to right across the bottom of the screen. Tap the Play button to preview the movie in real time in the Viewer.

To skim the timeline, swipe left or right. The playhead remains in the middle of the screen, so instead of positioning the playhead on the video, you're actually positioning the video clips under the playhead.

> **tip** On the iPhone or iPod touch, you can also swipe within the Viewer to skim the timeline. On the iPad, tap and hold the upper-left or upper-right corner of the timeline to quickly jump to the beginning or end.

Edit clips

After adding footage to the timeline, you'll find yourself moving, trimming, splitting, and deleting sections to cut out unwanted sections and create good timing. iMovie on the iPad 2 also has an abbreviated Precision Editor for fine-tuning the edit points between clips.

Moving a clip on the timeline

1. Tap and hold the clip you want to move. It lifts out of the timeline as a small thumbnail (**Figure 7.8**).

2. Without lifting your finger from the screen, drag the clip to a new location in the timeline.

Figure 7.8
Moving a clip in the timeline

Trimming a clip

1. Tap a clip once to reveal its selection handles.

2. Drag a handle to shorten or lengthen a clip (**Figure 7.9**).

Figure 7.9
Trimming a clip

tip   To view more thumbnails in the timeline, pinch outward horizontally with two fingers to expand the clips; pinch inward to compress the sizes of the clips.

Splitting a clip

1. Position the clip so the playhead is at the point where you want to split it.

2. Tap the clip to select it.

3. Slide one finger down the playhead from the top of the clip to the bottom (**Figure 7.10**). The clip is split into two, with a transition added between them. (The transition, however, is set to None, so there's no break between clips when you play the video. See "Edit transitions," on the next page.)

Figure 7.10
Splitting a clip

Deleting a clip

Drag a clip from the timeline to the Viewer until you see a small cloud icon appear (**Figure 7.11**). When you lift your finger from the screen, the clip disappears in a puff of smoke.

Figure 7.11
Giving a clip the
Keyser Söze treatment

Using the Precision Editor

1. On the iPad 2, tap a transition icon to select it and then tap the double-triangle icon to display the Precision Editor (**Figure 7.12**). Or, pinch outward vertically on a transition.

Figure 7.12
The Precision Editor

2. Do any of the following to adjust the edit point:

   • Drag the transition itself to reposition the edit point without changing the duration of the surrounding clips.

   • Drag the top handle to change the end point of the previous clip, without adjusting the next clip.

   • Drag the bottom handle to change the start point of the next clip without adjusting the previous clip.

 It's not possible to adjust the duration of the transition from within the Precision Editor. For that you need to edit the transition itself.

3. Tap the triangle icons, or pinch two fingers together, to close the Precision Editor.

Edit transitions

Whether you like it or not, iMovie automatically adds transitions between every clip. Now, before your imagination fills with endless cross dissolves, note that it's possible to have a transition that doesn't do anything at all. In other words, iMovie adds a transition placeholder between every clip so you don't have to drag one from elsewhere.

Editing transitions

1. Double-tap a transition icon to reveal the Transition Settings window (**Figure 7.13**).

Figure 7.13
Choosing a transition style and duration

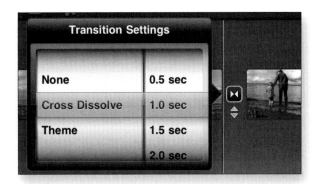

2. At the left side of the window, scroll to choose the type of transition: None (creating an abrupt jump cut between the clips on either side), Cross Dissolve, or Theme.

   The appearance of the latter depends on which theme you chose for your project. To change the theme, tap the Project Settings button and highlight a new one, as described earlier in the chapter.

3. At the right side of the window, scroll to choose one of the four preset durations for the transition.

4. To apply the changes, tap outside the window to dismiss it on an iPad 2; on an iPhone or iPod touch, tap the Done button.

Add a title

Like transitions, titles do not exist in a separate pane, ready to be dragged onto a clip. Instead, any clip can have a title, which is an attribute of the clip, not something added separately.

Adding a title

1. Double-tap a clip to view the Clip Settings window (**Figure 7.14**).

Figure 7.14
The Clip Settings window

2. Tap the Title Style button; the default style is None.

3. Choose a title style: Opening, Middle, or Ending. The styles depend on the project's theme, and are designed for common spots in your movie. For example, Opening is good for titles at the start of a movie and can occupy the entire screen, while Middle typically runs a title at the bottom of the screen without obscuring your video. Of course, you can choose whichever style you want at any point in your movie.

4. Tap the text field in the Viewer and enter your title text (**Figure 7.15**).

5. Tap Done in the virtual keyboard to stop editing the title.

Figure 7.15
Entering text in a theme title

Adding a title to just a portion of a clip

A title spans the entire length of a clip—even if the clip is several minutes long. If you want the title to appear on just a portion, such as the first few seconds, do the following:

1. Position the playhead in the clip where you want the title to end.

2. Split the clip.

3. Double-click the portion you want and add a title to it.

Specify a location

The iPhone, iPad 2, and iPod touch can all embed location data in the photos and video they capture, thanks to their built-in assisted-GPS technologies. iMovie reads that data, too, and gives you the option of using it in titles and, creatively, a few themes.

Specifying a location

1. Double-tap a clip to bring up the Clip Settings window.

2. Tap the Location button.

3. If location information was saved with the clip, it appears in the Location window (**Figure 7.16**). To change the location, do one of the following:

   • To use your current location, tap the crosshairs button.

   • To find a location, tap the Other button to search iMovie's database of locations. Tap the closest match to use it.

Figure 7.16
Location settings

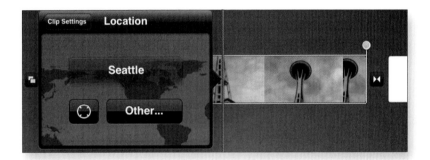

4. You can also change the label to something more specific, like a neighborhood or restaurant name. Tap the label and enter new text. It won't change the underlying location data. For example, the Travel theme adds a location marker to a map in its Opening title; the marker stays in place, but its label changes (**Figure 7.17**).

Figure 7.17
A custom label applied to the location data

5. To exit the Clip Settings window, tap outside it (iPad 2) or tap the Done button (iPhone and iPod touch).

In most themes, the location appears as a subhead below the title. If you don't want to announce the location, why not put that text to good use? In the Location window, enter any text you wish to display, even if it has nothing to do with location (Figure 7.18).

Figure 7.18
Use the Location line as a subhead.

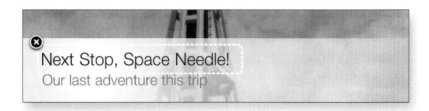

As you're working on editing your movie, you can tap the Undo button to reverse the last action; on the iPhone or iPod touch, shake the device to display the Undo button. But what if you tap Undo a few too many times? On the iPad, tap and hold the Undo button, which reveals a Redo button; on the iPhone and iPod touch, Redo appears with Undo when you shake the device.

Add and Edit Photos

Predictably, iMovie for iOS can import photos as well as video, and even manages to apply the Ken Burns Effect to them. In fact, every photo gets the Ken Burns treatment, without an easy way to keep an imported photo from moving.

Import photos from the Photos app

Photos you've shot using the device or that were synced from your computer can be brought into your iMovie project. As with video, if you captured photos from within iMovie, those images are restricted to the project that was active when you did the shooting.

If you shot photos using your iPhone or iPod touch, you can transfer them directly to an iPad using Apple's iPad Camera Connection Kit. See "Import from a camera, iPhone, or iPod touch," earlier in this chapter.

Importing photos

1. Position the playhead in the timeline where you want a new photo to appear.

 2. Go to the Media Library and tap the Photos button to view available photo albums.

3. Tap an album name to view its photos (**Figure 7.19**).

4. To preview a photo, tap and hold its thumbnail. On the iPad 2 in landscape orientation, the preview appears in the Viewer. On other devices, a larger version of the image floats above the album.

5. Tap the photo thumbnail once to add it to the timeline.

Edit the Ken Burns Effect

If you recall from Chapter 4, the Ken Burns Effect is based on the position of the frame at the beginning and end of the clip. iMovie determines how best to make the camera move from one state to the other.

Editing the Ken Burns Effect settings

1. In the timeline, tap a photo you've imported to select it.

2. Tap the Start button to move the playhead to the first frame of the clip (**Figure 7.20**).

Figure 7.20
Editing Ken Burns
Effects on the iPhone

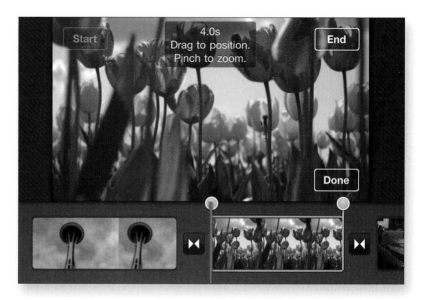

3. Position the starting frame the way you wish: Pinch inward or outward to zoom in on, or out of, the frame.

4. Tap the End button to move the playhead to the last frame of the clip.

5. Adjust the image to the way you want it to appear at the end of the sequence.

6. Tap Done to finish editing the Ken Burns Effect.

Disabling the Ken Burns Effect

Unfortunately, there's no easy control to turn off the Ken Burns Effect and just display a static photo. However, it is possible.

1. Tap the Start button.

2. Pinch the image on screen so you can see all of its edges (zoomed out) and then release it—iMovie snaps it back into place with a minimal amount of zoom applied.

3. Tap the End button and repeat step 2 to let iMovie snap it into place.

4. Tap Done to stop editing the photo.

Edit Audio

One area where iMovie for iOS sacrifices features for mobility is in editing audio. You can adjust the volume level for an entire clip, not specific levels within the clip; it's also not possible to detach audio from a video clip. Still, that leaves plenty of functionality, especially now that you can add multiple background music clips, include up to three additional sound effects at a time, and record voiceovers.

 When working with audio on the iPad 2, it's extremely helpful to view audio waveforms on tracks; the feature isn't available on the iPhone or iPod touch. Tap the Audio Waveforms button to make them visible.

Change a clip's volume level

So you don't have multiple audio sources fighting for attention, you can adjust the volume level for any clip, or mute it entirely.

Changing a clip's volume level

1. Double-tap a clip in the timeline to display the Clip Settings window.

2. Drag the volume slider to increase or decrease the overall level (**Figure 7.21**). To mute, tap the On/Off switch so it's set to Off.

Figure 7.21
Change a clip's volume in the Clip Settings window.

Volume slider

Add background music

For the easiest approach, iMovie can include background music, designed for the current theme, that loops in the background. Or, you can add your own audio tracks (with a few limitations). As with iMovie on the Mac, a project can have a background music track that operates a bit differently than other audio tracks. In the iOS version, a song in the background starts at the beginning of the movie; it can't be pinned to a specific location in the movie.

Adding automatic theme music

1. Tap the Project Settings button.

2. Tap the Theme Music switch so it's set to On. (The Loop Background Music option is automatically enabled.)

3. Tap outside the Project Settings window (iPad) or tap the Done button (iPhone and iPod touch) to apply the setting.

Adding a background music clip

1. Go to the Media Library and tap the Audio button.

2. Choose an audio source (**Figure 7.22**). In addition to iMovie's theme music selections, the Audio window gives you access to your iTunes music library, sorted by playlists, albums, artists, or songs.

Figure 7.22
The Audio window

3. Tap the name of a song to add it to your project. It appears as a green track behind the video clips in the timeline (**Figure 7.23**).

Music written for each theme is available to add to any project, not just to movies with those themes. In the Audio library, tap Theme Music and choose any song you wish.

Figure 7.23
A background
song added to
the timeline

4. To add multiple background songs that play one after another, go to the Project Settings window and disable the Loop Background Music option. You can then add more audio clips. If you don't change that project setting, iMovie replaces any background song when you add a new one.

 iMovie does not import any music encumbered with Apple's FairPlay DRM scheme; those tracks appear in the song list, but in gray with "(Protected)" before their names. Apple abandoned DRM for music tracks a while ago, but you may still have tracks in your iTunes library from before the switch. If you still want to use a specific song, go to iTunes on your computer, click iTunes Store in the sidebar, and then click the iTunes Plus link under Quick Links. That gives you the option to upgrade protected songs (for a fee of $0.30 per song, or 30 percent of an album's current price) to the DRM-free iTunes Plus format.

 iMovie considers any audio file less than one minute in length to be a sound effect, and won't add it as a background song.

Aside from the fact that a background song can't be repositioned in the timeline, you can edit it like most clips. Tap to select it and adjust its duration using the selection handles, or double-tap it to adjust the clip's overall volume.

One downside is that you can't apply a fade to an audio clip, so if you shorten the clip, the audio ends abruptly.

 Whenever a video clip with audio appears over a background song, the song is automatically ducked (made softer). Unfortunately, iMovie offers no controls for specifying the amount of ducking to apply.

Add a sound effect

When you want to add a little punch to your audio, consider throwing in a sound effect. Up to three sound effect clips can appear in a section at a time.

Adding a sound effect

1. Position the playhead at the section where you want a sound effect to start.

2. In the Media Library, tap the Audio button.

3. Tap the Sound Effects button to view a list of available effects.

4. Tap the name of the effect you want to use. It's added to the timeline (**Figure 7.24**).

Figure 7.24
The Water Splash sound effect is added to coincide with a splash in the video.

> **tip** Using iMovie's audio recording feature, you can record sound effects while you're shooting or anywhere else. See "Add a voiceover" on the next page.

> **tip** iMovie's automatic assumption that any audio clip less than one minute in length is a sound effect is an annoyance when you want to use a short song to open your movie. But it's also an advantage: You can add any music file—whether its content is a sound effect or not—that's under one minute as a sound effect clip.

Add a voiceover

Most of the time, your videos can speak for themselves. On occasion, though, you may want to provide narration or a commentary track that plays over the footage. iMovie's audio import feature lets you record your voice (or any sound, for that matter) into the timeline.

Adding a voiceover

1. Position the playhead in your movie where you want to begin recording audio.

2. Tap the Record button to bring up the Ready to Record window.

3. When you're ready to start capturing audio, tap the Record button in the window. iMovie counts down from 3 to 1 and then begins recording (**Figure 7.25**).

Figure 7.25
Recording a voiceover

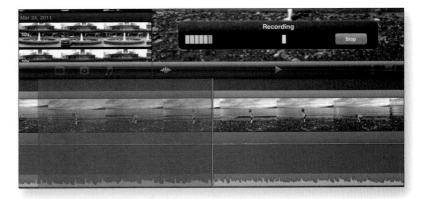

4. Tap the Stop button to end recording. The recorded clip appears as a purple audio clip below the video in the timeline.

5. Choose what to do with the recorded clip: Tap Review to listen to it; tap Retake to record again; tap Discard to delete the recording; or tap Accept to keep it in your project (**Figure 7.26**).

Figure 7.26
Review your recording before adding it to the timeline.

Feel free to record multiple takes, but keep in mind that you can have only three audio tracks in one spot at a time. Also, mute the other takes before you record a new one.

 To capture better-quality audio, consider using a microphone instead of relying on the device's built-in mic. That can be the microphone on the earbuds that come with the iPhone or even, when connected to the iPad using the iPad Camera Connection Kit, a professional microphone or USB headset.

Share Projects

iMovie for iOS is designed to easily turn footage into a movie, but it's also intended to take your video and share it with the world. That could mean saving the finished movie to the Camera Roll for later viewing or for importing into iTunes on your computer, or sending it directly to YouTube, Facebook, Vimeo, or CNN iReport.

Share to the Camera Roll

When you share your project to the Camera Roll, a final version of the movie is created and made available for you to not only watch, but access from other apps with access to your photo and video library, such as Keynote.

Sharing to the Camera Roll

1. Tap the My Projects button to return to the opening screen.

2. With the project you want to share highlighted front and center, tap the Share button (**Figure 7.27**).

3. Tap the Camera Roll button.

4. In the next dialog, choose a resolution to export: Medium (360p), Large (540p), or HD (720p). iMovie creates the finished movie and saves it to the Camera Roll.

5. To view the movie, open the Photos app, locate the movie at the bottom of the Photos list, and tap the Play button.

Figure 7.27
Share menu options

To upload a finished movie to your MobileMe Gallery, share it to the Camera Roll first. From there, you can open the movie, tap the Action button, and choose Send to MobileMe.

Share to YouTube, Facebook, Vimeo, or CNN iReport

With an Internet connection, you can upload your video directly to a sharing service that publishes the work online almost instantly—you don't need to sync with a computer first.

Sharing to YouTube, Facebook, Vimeo, or CNN iReport

1. At the My Projects screen, highlight the movie you want to export.

2. Tap the Share menu to bring up the list of destinations.

3. Tap the button for the service you want to use. (I'm presuming you already have an account with one or more of them; if not, you'll need to go sign up for one on the Web.)

4. If prompted, enter your login information.

5. Enter a title and description in the fields provided (**Figure 7.28**, on the next page).

6. Tap the Category field and specify one of the categories.

7. Choose a size to create for uploading.

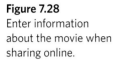

Figure 7.28
Enter information
about the movie when
sharing online.

8. Set the privacy level to control who can view the movie.

9. Tap the Share button when you're ready to proceed. iMovie prepares
    the movie and uploads it.

    When finished, iMovie gives you the option of viewing the movie on
    the Web or sharing the location in an outgoing email message.

Send the project to another device via iTunes

Another method of sharing an iMovie project is, quite frankly, a weird
workaround. It's possible to export the project itself, not just a rendered
version of the movie, for backing up to your Mac or sending to another
iOS device for editing. (Sadly, at this time you can't bring your iMovie
for iOS project and finish editing it in iMovie on the Mac. Someday, I
hope.) It is, however, a fairly counterintuitive procedure.

Exporting a project to iTunes

1. At the My Projects screen, highlight the project you wish to export
    and tap the Share button.

2. Tap the Send Project to iTunes button. iMovie packages all the data and resources (including video clips and audio files) and then informs you when the export is complete.

3. Connect your iPad, iPhone, or iPod touch to your computer.

4. Open iTunes and select the device in the sidebar.

5. Click the Apps button at the top of the screen and scroll down to the File Sharing section.

6. Select iMovie in the Apps column.

7. Select the project you exported (**Figure 7.29**) and click the Save To button. Specify a location, such as the Desktop.

Figure 7.29
The exported project in iTunes

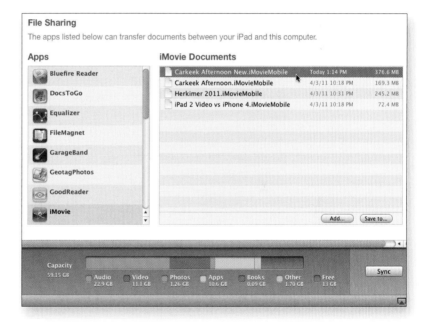

Importing the project into iMovie on another iOS device

1. Connect the other device to iTunes and select it in the sidebar.

2. Go to the Apps screen, scroll down to the File Sharing section, and select iMovie in the Apps column.

3. Click the Add button and locate the project file you exported above. Or, drag the project from the Finder to the iMovie Documents

column. (You don't need to sync the device to copy the file; it's added directly.)

4. Open iMovie on the device.

5. Although the project now exists on the device, iMovie doesn't yet know about it. Go to the My Projects screen and tap the Import button.

6. In the dialog that appears, tap the name of the project to import it. It appears among your other projects (**Figure 7.30**).

See? Only 13 steps to move a project from one device to another!

Figure 7.30
Importing the "Carkeek Afternoon New" project into iMovie on an iPhone

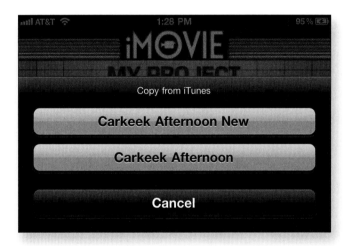

This method is also a way to duplicate a project—for example, if you want to save what you've done but try an editing experiment. After sharing to iTunes, tap the Import button to bring a copy back in; it will have a slightly different name.

Index